AUSTRIA

TRAVEL GUIDE 2025

JANICE DENISON

Copyright © 2025 by Janice Denison.

All rights reserved.

No part of this publication may be reproduced, distributed, or transmitted in any form or by any means, including photocopying, recording, or other electronic or mechanical methods, without the prior written permission of the publisher, except in the case of brief quotations embodied in critical reviews and certain other noncommercial uses permitted by copyright law.

Disclaimer

This guide is intended for informational purposes only. Please be aware that it does not include any images, as the book is printed in black and white. While the guide provides in-depth descriptions of the places you may visit, I recommend checking platforms like Instagram or other social media outlets for up-to-date photos of the locations and attractions.

All costs mentioned in this guide are estimates and may vary. I encourage you to confirm prices for lodging, transportation, and attractions in advance to avoid any surprises during your trip.

TABLE OF CONTENTS

INTRODUCTION 7
GETTING STARTED 8
   Overview of Austria 8
   Why Visit Austria in 2025? 9
   How to Use This Guide 11
HISTORY AND CULTURE 13
   Early History 13
   The Habsburg Empire 14
   Modern Austria 16
AUSTRIAN CULTURE & TRADITIONS 19
   Language and Dialects 19
   Festivals and Holidays 21
   Music, Art, and Literature 23
   Austrian Etiquette & Customs 26
TRAVEL CHECKLIST 29
   Essential Documents 29
   Packing Tips 31
   Travel Insurance 33
WHEN TO VISIT 36
   Best Time of Year 36
   Seasonal Highlights 38
GETTING THERE 42
   By Air 42
   By Train 44

By Car 47

GETTING AROUND 51

    Public Transportation 51

    Driving in Austria 53

    Cycling and Walking 56

VIENNA: THE IMPERIAL CITY 59

    Must-See Attractions 61

    Best Areas to Stay 65

    Shopping in Vienna 68

    Nightlife and Entertainment 70

    Exploring Vienna 73

SALZBURG: THE CITY OF MOZART 76

    Historical Sites and Museums 76

    Salzburg's Music Scene 79

    Where to Stay 81

    Outdoor Activities 83

    Exploring Salzburg 87

INNSBRUCK: THE HEART OF THE ALPS 90

    Ski Resorts and Winter Sports 90

    Summer Activities 93

    Best Areas to Stay 98

    Cultural Sites 100

    Exploring Innsbruck 104

GRAZ: AUSTRIA'S CULINARY CAPITAL 107

    Historical and Modern Attractions 107

  Best Places to Stay 110

  Exploring Graz 113

OTHER NOTABLE DESTINATIONS 116

  Hallstatt 116

  Zell am See 117

  Klagenfurt 119

  Linz 122

OUTDOOR ADVENTURES 125

  Hiking and Mountaineering 125

  Skiing and Snowboarding 127

  Watersports 129

  Cycling Trails 132

CULTURAL AND HISTORICAL TOURS 136

  Castles and Palaces 136

  Museums and Galleries 140

  Historical Walking Tours 145

WINE AND DINE 150

  Austrian Cuisine Overview 150

  Top Restaurants across Austria 152

  Wine Regions and Tours 157

FESTIVALS AND EVENTS 160

  Major Annual Festivals 160

  Local Celebrations 162

  Music and Arts Festivals 166

ACCOMMODATION OPTIONS 170

 Hotels and Resorts 170

 Budget Lodging 174

 Unique Stays 179

HEALTH AND SAFETY 183

 Medical Services and Emergencies 183

 Safety Tips for Travelers 186

MONEY MATTERS 189

 Currency and Exchange 189

 Budgeting Tips 191

 Sample Budget 193

LANGUAGE AND PHRASES 196

 Basic German Phrases 196

 Language Resources 198

DAY TRIPS AND EXCURSIONS 199

 From Vienna to Wachau Valley 199

 From Salzburg to Hallstatt 200

 From Innsbruck to Neuschwanstein Castle 202

CONCLUSION 204

APPENDIX 205

GLOSSARY 209

INTRODUCTION

Welcome, fellow traveler! I'm pleased you've decided to join me on this tour around Austria. In case you're an experienced traveler or planning your first trip, Austria will capture your heart and soul.

Envision yourself roaming around Vienna's vast imperial castles, taking in Salzburg's musical legacy, or skiing down the breathtaking slopes of the Austrian Alps. Austria is a nation where history and modernity combine perfectly, providing diverse experiences for all types of travelers.

This book has everything you need to make the most of your Austrian vacation. We'll visit the country's vibrant culture, breathtaking scenery, and lovely cities and villages. I've got you covered, from the best places to eat delicious Austrian cuisine to hidden gems off the beaten track.

Expect practical advice to help you plan your trip efficiently, thorough recommendations for must-see attractions, and personal anecdotes that bring the destinations to life. I created this book to be your trusted companion, providing insights and guidance as if we were sitting together, creating your ideal itinerary over coffee.

So, let us get started! Austria welcomes you with open arms, eager to share its wonders. Enjoy your adventure!

GETTING STARTED

Overview of Austria

Welcome to Austria, a region of enduring allure and stunning beauty! Nestled in the heart of Europe, Austria seamlessly weaves together a rich tapestry of history, culture, and stunning scenery. From its breathtaking Alpine peaks to its scenic valleys and vibrant cities, Austria has a plethora of experiences that guarantee to captivate and inspire.

Envision wandering through Vienna's majestic streets, past imperial palaces and beautiful coffee shops that reflect the Habsburg Empire's grandeur. Feel the magic in Salzburg, Mozart's birthplace, where music fills the air and baroque architecture reveals stories from centuries before. Experience the excitement of adventure in Innsbruck, where the towering Alps beckon you to ski, trek, and explore.

However, Austria is more than its famed cities. It's a region where historic mountain villages greet visitors warmly, where the splendor of the Danube River spreads along gorgeous pathways, and where every corner appears to have a piece of history waiting to be discovered. The country's rich vineyards, quiet lakes, and picturesque landscapes are ideal for people seeking peace and a deeper connection with nature.

As you plan your trip, this guide will be your companion, providing information on the top sites, hidden jewels, and local treats. We'll explore Austria's lively cultural landscape, sample its culinary delicacies, and learn about the customs that make this country unique.

Why Visit Austria in 2025?

New attractions

1. Vienna's Contemporary Arts Hub

Vienna has launched a brand-new contemporary art hub that will showcase the works of established and rising artists. This dynamic location has rotating exhibitions, interactive installations, and art workshops, making it a must-see for art lovers. Check visit the outdoor sculpture garden for a stroll around fascinating artworks.

2. The Salzburg Musical Heritage Museum

Music enthusiasts will thrill at Salzburg's newly opened Musical Heritage Museum. This interactive museum explores the city's rich musical heritage, featuring exhibits on Mozart, the Salzburg Festival, and Austria's classical music legacy. This exciting addition to Salzburg's cultural landscape features interactive displays and live performances.

Exciting events

1. The Innsbruck Winter Sports Festival

In January 2025, Innsbruck will hold its Winter Sports Festival, a week-long celebration of everything winter sports. This festival promises family fun with snowboarding competitions, ice sculpting contests, and cozy après-ski parties. Take advantage of the opportunity to participate in traditional Tyrolean winter activities.

2. The Vienna International Film Festival

The Vienna International Film Festival is back with a bang, presenting a wide roster of films worldwide. This year's festival will feature more outdoor screenings, panel talks with filmmakers, and special activities celebrating Austrian cinema. This is an excellent opportunity to engage oneself in the world of movies.

New dining experiences

1. EcoBite In Graz

Graz welcomes EcoBite, a sustainable dining concept making a splash in the culinary world. EcoBite, which focuses on locally sourced, organic products and inventive plant-based recipes, provides a new perspective on Austrian cuisine. The restaurant's rooftop garden provides many herbs and vegetables used in their recipes, offering a genuine farm-to-table experience.

2. Vienna Urban Food Market

Vienna's new Urban Food Market has rapidly become a popular destination for locals and tourists. This bustling market has many food stalls serving anything from traditional Austrian nibbles to foreign street food. It's ideal for a relaxing supper or trying out various dishes. Be sure to sample the freshly baked pretzels and specialty cheeses.

Significant changes

1. Increased Public Transportation in Salzburg

Salzburg has increased its public transportation network, making it easier to go around the city and its surroundings. The new tram lines and bus routes connect significant sites and neighborhoods, providing visitors a smooth travel experience. Deploying environmentally friendly electric buses also reflects the city's dedication to sustainability.

2. Vienna's Green Space Initiative

Vienna has initiated a citywide campaign to improve its green spaces, including more parks, urban gardens, and pedestrian-friendly places.

This program not only beautifies the city but also expands recreational opportunities for both inhabitants and visitors. The new riverside park along the Danube is a peaceful place to picnic, jog, or enjoy the scenery.

How to Use This Guide

First and foremost, start with the introduction. You'll be greeted warmly and given an overview of what makes Austria remarkable. This section sets the tone for your adventure, providing an overview of what to expect and emphasizing the special characteristics of Austria that you won't want to miss.

The guide is divided into clear, easy-to-follow parts, each focused on a different facet of your vacation. The History and Culture part will provide a comprehensive overview of Austria's past and present, allowing you to better understand the context of the places you'll see. Understanding the local culture will help you have better interactions and experiences on your vacation.

The Travel Essentials section is your practical toolkit. Here, you'll discover helpful hints for planning your trip, such as a travel checklist, advice on the best times to visit, and directions on how to get there and about. This section is intended to make your preparation process as seamless as possible, ensuring that you have covered all of the bases before you arrive in Austria.

As you progress through the guide, you will encounter in-depth sections on Austria's best destinations. Each city or region, from Vienna to Innsbruck, is assigned its chapter. These sections feature must-see sights, the greatest places to stay, top restaurants, shopping destinations, and nightlife. Each site is brought to life with vivid descriptions and personal recommendations, making you feel like you are traveling with a local friend.

The Experiences and Activities section is full of suggestions for what to do while you're there. This section of the guide contains thorough information and practical advice for anyone interested in outdoor experiences, cultural and historical trips, and sampling local food. It's ideal for folks who enjoy planning their activities ahead of time, ensuring they don't miss anything.

Further on, the Practical Information section discusses lodging possibilities, health and safety precautions, money matters, language phrases, and shopping. This guide section assists you with day-to-day logistics, ensuring your stay is as comfortable and convenient as possible. It's like having a local expert ready to assist whenever needed.

For those wishing to travel beyond the main tourist attractions, the Exploring Beyond the Cities section recommends day trips and hidden gems. Here, you'll find ideas for off-the-beaten-path activities and lesser-known sites that provide a more personal glimpse of Austria.

Keep the guide with you for fast reference when traveling. The clear headings and subheadings make it simple to discover the information you need, if you're seeking a restaurant recommendation or guidance on using public transportation. The practical advice and personal experiences in this guide will enrich your trip and help you connect with Austria on a deeper level.

This book is more than simply a list of facts; it's a helpful companion on your journey. It's written conversational to put you at ease and get you enthusiastic about your vacation. Use it as a route map, advisor, and source of inspiration. With this book in hand, you're ready for an unforgettable journey to Austria. Enjoy your travels!

HISTORY AND CULTURE

Early History

Austria's history is like a tapestry, with bright threads of significant events, influential personalities, and long-standing cultural traditions.

Our voyage begins with the ancient Celts, who were among the first to settle in what is now known as Austria, approximately 400 BC. These early colonists were expert metalworkers and dealers, producing stunning artifacts that reveal much about their way of life. Consider bustling Celtic settlements, where the sounds of hammers shaping metal and vibrant markets fill the air.

Fast-forward to the Roman Empire, when Austria was referred to as Noricum. The Romans arrived in 15 BC, and their impact is still seen today. They constructed remarkable highways, villages, and fortifications, laying the groundwork for many modern Austrian cities. Carnuntum, located near present-day Vienna, was a major Roman settlement. Walking amid its ruins, one can almost hear the sounds of Roman troops and merchants going about their everyday business.

The fall of the Roman Empire ushered in a time of upheaval, with different Germanic tribes, including the Bavarians, coming into the region. By the eighth century, Charlemagne, the great Frankish ruler, had gained control and included Austria in his huge kingdom. During this time, Christianity flourished, and monasteries arose, important in preserving knowledge and culture.

Now, let us discuss the Babenbergs, the dynasty that laid the groundwork for modern Austria. Beginning in the late 10th century, the Babenbergs played an important role in the region's development. They transformed Vienna into a major political and cultural hub.

Envision a medieval city with guarded walls, busy markets, and grand cathedrals.

The Babenberg era paved the way for establishing one of Europe's most powerful families, the Habsburgs. The Habsburg family established its power in the 13th century and would alter Austria for centuries. Rudolph I, the first Habsburg monarch, played a significant role in establishing the dynasty's dominance. Under Habsburg's reign, Austria grew substantially, becoming a major participant in European affairs.

During these early centuries, Austria's cultural traditions also developed. Folk music, dances, and festivals flourished, reflecting the different influences of the Celts, Romans, and Germanic tribes. Consider the lively tunes of traditional Austrian folk music, with people dancing in colorful costumes to honor their rich heritage.

The Habsburg Empire

Envision we're sitting in one of Vienna's stately coffee houses, the perfume of freshly made coffee in the air, as we learn about the intriguing history of the Habsburg Empire. The Habsburgs were more than just rulers; they shaped Austria's golden period, leaving an enduring imprint on the country's identity and culture.

Our tale begins in the 13th century, with Rudolph I, the first Habsburg monarch of Germany, who laid the groundwork for the dynasty's rise to power. Rudolph secured Austrian territory in 1278, following a decisive fight at Marchfeld, ushering in Habsburg domination. Consider the medieval landscape as the Habsburgs began to spread their power through clever marriages and alliances, gradually expanding their possessions throughout Europe.

By the 16th century, the Habsburgs had established themselves as a strong force. Charles V, one of the most famous Habsburg kings, ruled over a never-ending empire that included large areas in Europe and the Americas. Charles V's reign was characterized by grandeur and upheaval as he negotiated religious tensions and political obstacles. Envision his court, full of advisors, artists, and diplomats from all across the world.

Empress Maria Theresa, who governed in the 18th century, was one of the Habsburgs' most powerful figures. She was more than a monarch; she was also a reformer who altered Austria. Maria Theresa's rule brought considerable changes, including educational reforms, economic expansion, and military advances. Consider her a committed leader who balances her obligations as a mother of sixteen and ruler of a vast kingdom. Her contributions paved the way for modern Austria, making her a renowned figure in Austrian history.

The Habsburgs were tremendous benefactors of the arts, sparking a cultural revolution that continues today. Vienna grew as a center of music, art, and architecture during their control. Consider the grandeur of the Vienna State Opera, where works by Mozart, Beethoven, and Haydn first enthralled audiences. The exquisite Schönbrunn and Hofburg Palaces, testaments to the Habsburgs' history, reflect their love of Baroque and Rococo design.

A history of the Habsburgs is incomplete without including Franz Joseph I, who governed from 1848 to 1916. His reign, one of the longest in European history, was highlighted by key events like the Austro-Hungarian Compromise of 1867, which established Austria-Hungary as a dual monarchy. Consider Franz Joseph a firm hand throughout stormy times, keeping the empire stable despite wars and political turmoil.

The assassination of Archduke Franz Ferdinand, a key Habsburg figure, in 1914 set off a chain of events that led to World War I, which marked the end of the Habsburg Empire. By 1918, the once-mighty empire had collapsed, signaling the end of Habsburg sovereignty. Envision the anguish and turmoil as Austria moved from an imperial powerhouse to a republic, irreversibly altering its course.

Even though the Habsburg Empire is no longer, its legacy endures. The traditions, cultural achievements, and architectural marvels they left behind continue to influence Austria's identity. The Habsburgs have left an indelible mark on Austrian life, from vast palaces and towering churches to the enduring influence of classical music.

As you visit Austria, you'll encounter numerous reminders of this illustrious family. Each castle, museum, and music theater depicts a time when the Habsburgs reigned with majesty and vision. It's like wandering through history, encountering the remnants of an empire that shaped not only Austria but the entire world.

Modern Austria

Let's take a trip through Vienna's vibrant streets, where the past and present merge seamlessly, and discover what makes modern Austria such an interesting and dynamic city. Austria, with its dynamic cultural scene and forward-thinking inventions, is a country that has embraced its heritage while looking boldly to the future.

Our adventure began after World War I when the once-mighty Habsburg Empire collapsed, and Austria became a republic in 1918. This changeover was difficult, as Austria faced economic hardships and political upheaval. Consider the Austrian people's tenacity as they rebuilt their country from the ruins of an empire.

The annexation by Nazi Germany in 1938, as well as the devastation of World War II, added to the difficulties of the twentieth century. Austria's cities, particularly Vienna, bore the marks of conflict.

Following the war, the Allied forces ruled Austria until 1955, when the Austrian State Treaty was signed, restoring Austria's freedom and establishing its eternal neutrality. Envision the relief and hope as Austrians began rebuilding again, building the groundwork for a peaceful and prosperous future.

Austria experienced a postwar economic miracle. Thanks to Marshall Plan aid and its people's hard work, Austria became a strong economy. By the 1960s, Austria was among the world's wealthiest countries. Envision thriving industry, expanding cities, and a country that embraces modernity while preserving its cultural legacy.

In 1995, Austria joined the European Union, an important milestone in its modern history. This step not only strengthened Austria's position in Europe but also resulted in economic growth and greater international cooperation. Today, Austria is an important member of the EU, contributing to and benefiting from the region's overall prosperity and security.

Modern Austria is a cultural powerhouse, with Vienna being dubbed the "City of Music" for its continual contributions to the arts. The Vienna Philharmonic Orchestra, the annual Vienna Opera Ball, and the numerous music festivals are examples of Austria's rich musical legacy. Consider attending a classical concert in one of Vienna's historic venues, where the notes of Mozart and Beethoven echo through time.

The arts include more than just music. Austria's museums, galleries, and theaters are brimming with activity. The Albertina, Belvedere, and Kunsthistorisches Museums in Vienna have magnificent art collections that attract visitors worldwide. Envision meandering through these halls, surrounded by centuries-old artworks.

In the twenty-first century, Austria has established itself as a pioneer in innovation and sustainability. The country is well-known for its technological advances, renewable energy, and environmental protection. Austria's dedication to green energy is demonstrated by its considerable usage of hydropower and pioneering work in solar and wind energy. Envision a landscape dotted with environmentally friendly efforts, such as energy-efficient buildings and sustainable transportation systems.

Austrian cities are also hubs of innovation. Vienna, in particular, is routinely recognized as one of the world's most livable cities, owing to its superior infrastructure, high quality of life, and emphasis on sustainability. Envision a city where modernity and green living coexist, providing residents and visitors with a good standard of living.

Modern Austria is a cultural melting pot, with an increasing immigrant population contributing to the country's social and cultural fabric. This diversity is evident in Austria's culinary scene, festivals, and daily life. Envision crowded marketplaces with tastes from around the world and colorful multicultural events honoring Austrian society's unique tapestry.

Today, Austria is a country that values its past while looking forward. Austria's stunning Alpine communities and vibrant urban hubs uniquely combine tradition and innovation.

AUSTRIAN CULTURE & TRADITIONS

Language and Dialects

Austria's official language is German. But don't be fooled into believing this is the same German spoken in Berlin or Hamburg. Austrian German, or Österreichisches Deutsch, has its distinct style and flavor. Consider it a dialect formed only inside Austria's boundaries, with words and phrases that are unmistakably Austrian.

For example, when ordering breakfast, you can request a "Semmel" (a bread roll) rather than a "Brötchen," as is common in Germany. And if you're having a festive meal, you might be served "Marillen" (apricots) instead of "Aprikosen." These minor changes provide a pleasant local flavor to the language, making interactions in Austria warm and comfortable.

Austria's regional dialects reflect the country's linguistic variety. Traveling across the country, you'll encounter various accents and vocabulary. Each location has a particular dialect influenced by history, geography, and culture.

In Vienna, for example, the Viennese dialect, often known as Wienerisch, is a musical, occasionally sing-song variety of German. It's noted for its endearing remarks and distinctive pronunciation. Envision yourself strolling through Vienna's crowded marketplaces, hearing vendors cry out in their unique Viennese tones, adding to the city's dynamic ambiance.

When you travel west to Tyrol, you'll come across Tyrolean dialects that sound very different from Viennese. These dialects are impacted by the region's hilly environment and historical ties to neighboring nations such as Italy. Envision chatting with a nice resident in

Innsbruck, where the speech is rhythmic and almost musical, reflecting the Alpine culture.

Salzburg's vocabulary has a sweet, pleasant lilt that stems from the city's strong musical legacy. As you wander Salzburg's old streets, you may find yourself humming along with the local accent, which appears to harmonize with the Mozart melodies that fill the air.

Austria's dialects reflect not only regional distinctions but also the country's rich history. Because of the Habsburg Empire's influence and its location at the crossroads of Central Europe, Austria has been a melting pot of cultures and languages for centuries.

The loanwords and idioms that have entered Austrian German reflect this historical tapestry. Words borrowed from Czech, Hungarian, and Italian are common, particularly in territories once part of the Austro-Hungarian Empire. These linguistic vestiges enrich and deepen how Austrians speak today, creating a magnificent mosaic of sound and meaning.

Modern Austria values linguistic diversity. With an increasing immigrant population, you'lla wide range of languages are spoken in cities and towns across the country. Turkish, Serbian, Croatian, and English are widely spoken, contributing to the varied linguistic landscape.

In Vienna, the multicultural capital, this diversity is especially evident. Walking through the city's districts, you'll come across communities speaking various languages, each adding to the cultural mosaic that makes Vienna so vibrant and global.

Understanding local dialects can be difficult, but it's part of the pleasure. Don't be afraid to inquire if you are unclear about a word or phrase. Austrians are often patient and willing to help, frequently switching to normal German or even English to facilitate conversation.

The beauty of Austria's language and dialects stems from their dynamic, developing nature. They are more than simply historical artifacts; they are an active part of modern life. Austria's linguistic diversity, from how locals chat in cafés to the unusual expressions you'll hear in markets and streets, reflects its rich cultural legacy.

Festivals and Holidays

Christmas Markets

One of the most magical experiences in Austria is visiting the Christmas markets, known as Christkindlmarkt. These markets, hosted in cities and villages around the country, convert the winter months into a magnificent wonderland. Envision wandering across Vienna's Rathausplatz, surrounded by dazzling lights, the aroma of roasted chestnuts in the air, and kiosks loaded with homemade ornaments, gifts, and holiday goodies.

Easter Celebrations

Easter in Austria is a time for colorful traditions and family gatherings. One of the most delightful traditions is the Easter market, which sells beautifully painted eggs, traditional crafts, and delectable pastries such as Osterpinze, a sweet bread. Envision youngsters on an Easter egg hunt, their joy filling the air as they look for hidden treasures in gardens and parks.

Fasching

Fasching, Austria's version of Carnival, is a vibrant event with parades, costumes, and parties. It usually takes place in February, before Lent. Envision the streets of Graz or Innsbruck filled with colorful floats, people dressed in elaborate costumes, and marching bands. It's a time for joy and celebration when communities celebrate with music, dance, and laughter.

Vienna Opera Ball

The Vienna Opera Ball is one of Austria's most prominent events, held every February at the Vienna State Opera. Envision an evening of elegance and splendor, with the main hall converted into a glittering ballroom. The guests, dressed in their finest gear, dance the night away to classical music. This event is a highlight of the social calendar, drawing people from all over the world.

Almabtrieb

In the autumn, the Almabtrieb celebration commemorates the return of livestock from alpine pastures to valleys. This celebration, conducted in rural places like Tyrol and Salzburg, is a colorful and joyful occasion. Envision gorgeously decorated cows parading through villages, their bells ringing, while inhabitants dress in traditional clothes and celebrate with music, dancing, and feasting.

Salzburg Festival

The Salzburg Festival, held each summer, is a world-renowned celebration of music and drama. This distinguished event, which began in 1920, features performances by some of the world's most talented performers. Envision watching an opera or play in Salzburg's historic streets, where large performances and intimate concerts bring the city's rich musical tradition to life.

National Day

Austria celebrates National Day on October 26th, the anniversary of the country's declaration of neutrality in 1955. This day celebrates national pride and unity, with festivities occurring nationwide. Consider flag-raising ceremonies, military parades, and open days at government facilities, where citizens and visitors can learn about Austria's history and achievements.

Krampusnacht

Krampusnacht, a unique and rather eerie festival, is observed on December 5th, the eve of Saint Nicholas Day in Austria. Krampus, a horned creature from legend, is thought to stalk the streets and punish naughty children. Envision the unnerving thrill of seeing people costumed as Krampus, complete with masks and costumes, marching through cities like Salzburg and Innsbruck. It's a strange mix of joy and terror, steeped in Alpine traditions.

Harvest Festivals

Harvest festivals, or Erntedankfeste, are held all over Austria in September and October to express gratitude for the year's bounty. These festivities include processions, music, traditional dances, and much food. Consider local communities gathering together, sharing meals, and expressing joy and thanks for the harvest.

New Year's Eve

Silvester, or New Year's Eve in Austria, is celebrated with spectacular fireworks, music, and dancing. In Vienna, the Vienna Philharmonic's New Year's Concert is a highlight transmitted to millions worldwide. Envision the excitement as the clock strikes midnight, fireworks light up the sky, and people raise glasses of sparkling champagne to toast the new year.

Music, Art, and Literature

The Sound of Music

Austria is commonly referred to as the "Land of Music," and with good cause. It produced some of the world's greatest composers. Consider Vienna in the 18th century, when the air was filled with the songs of Wolfgang Amadeus Mozart. Born in Salzburg, Mozart was a composer whose brilliance extended to operas, symphonies, and chamber music. Consider seeing a performance of "The Magic Flute" or "Don Giovanni," where each note appears to cast a magical spell.

Then there's Ludwig van Beethoven, who lived most of his life in Vienna. Despite his deafness, Beethoven wrote some of his most memorable works here, including the legendary Ninth Symphony with its "Ode to Joy." Envision the dramatic power of his symphonies ringing through magnificent concert halls, touching listeners' souls.

Franz Schubert, another Viennese treasure, was a master of lieder (German art songs). His music, filled with emotion and melody, frequently expressed the beauty and suffering of everyday life. Consider a calm evening in Vienna, listening to the gentle sounds of Schubert's "Ave Maria" or "Winterreise" and feeling the profound connection between music and human experience.

A Canvas for Creativity

Austria's contribution to the visual arts is equally impressive. Gustav Klimt pioneered the Secessionist movement, which broke away from traditional art styles at the turn of the twentieth century. Consider Klimt's masterwork, "The Kiss," with its golden hues and intricate patterns, which capture a moment of absolute intimacy and beauty. Like that of Egon Schiele and Oskar Kokoschka, his work questioned traditions and introduced new, expressive shapes into the spotlight.

Vienna's MuseumsQuartier is a powerhouse of cultural creation, featuring collections ranging from classical to modern art. Envision strolling through the Leopold Museum, where Schiele's expressive portraits and Kokoschka's dynamic compositions reveal Austrian art's revolutionary spirit.

The Albertina Museum in Vienna houses one of the world's most important collections of graphic art, including works by Albrecht Dürer, Leonardo da Vinci, and Michelangelo. Consider looking at Dürer's "Young Hare," marveling at the precise perfection and lifelike detail that bring the piece to life.

Literary Legends

Austria's literary legacy is brimming with voices that have shaped and reflected its cultural and historical setting. Franz Kafka was born in Prague but spent much of his life in Vienna. His writings, like "The Metamorphosis" and "The Trial," explore themes of existential dread and the absurdity of bureaucracy. Envision reading Kafka's weird stories and feeling the weight of his existential themes and the strange, frightening universe he built.

Stefan Zweig, a well-known Austrian writer of the early twentieth century, depicted the turbulent upheavals of his period in novels, biographies, and essays. His paintings, such as "The World of Yesterday," offer a sad glimpse into pre-World War II Europe, eliciting nostalgia and sorrow. Envision yourself absorbed in Zweig's elegant words, transported back to a beautiful and delicate world.

Elfriede Jelinek, a modern Austrian playwright and novelist, received the Nobel Prize in Literature in 2004. Her work frequently explores themes of gender, power, and societal oppression, forcing readers to confront uncomfortable realities. Consider watching a play by Jelinek, where her incisive dialogue and provocative ideas spark thought and discussion.

A Living Tradition

Austria'sIts thriving cultural scene today reflects a dedication to promoting the arts. Vienna's State Opera House remains a leading location for world-class performances, drawing music fans worldwide. Consider the elegance of an evening at the opera, the grandeur of the auditorium, and the moving performances that make it a memorable event.

The Salzburg Festival, held every summer, honors Austria's artistic legacy via opera, drama, and classical music. Envision Salzburg alive with the sounds of orchestras tuning, actors rehearsing, and crowds waiting for the next great performance.

Austrian Etiquette & Customs

Greetings and Introductions

In Austria, welcomes are considered a gesture of respect and courtesy. When meeting someone for the first time, it is normal to shake hands, keep eye contact, and smile warmly. This applies in both official and informal contexts. Consider yourself at a business meeting or a social gathering, where a strong handshake and a cordial "Grüß Gott" (a traditional greeting, particularly in rural areas) set the tone for a pleasant exchange.

In more casual settings, friends and family frequently greet one another with a quick kiss on the cheek, generally twice, beginning with the right cheek. This friendly gesture exemplifies the closeness of Austrian social relationships.

Table Manners

Dining in Austria is an experience to remember, and appropriate table manners are an important aspect of the culture. When invited to someone's home for a meal, it is normal to bring a little gift, such as flowers or a bottle of wine, to show appreciation. Envision walking into a quiet Austrian house, the delightful aroma of home-cooked food drifting through the air, and handing off your gift with a genuine "Danke schön."

When you arrive at the table, wait for the host to suggest where you should sit. When everyone is seated, waiting for the host to eat before you begin is courteous. Austrians value the art of conversation at meals, so take your time and enjoy both the cuisine and company. Envision having vibrant talks about local traditions while enjoying each meal course.

If you are dining out, remember to greet your fellow diners with "Mahlzeit" (enjoy your dinner) before you begin eating. This simple phrase is a way to wish everyone a good eating experience.

Coffeehouse Culture

Austrian coffee houses are cultural institutions where individuals can rest, read, and engage in meaningful conversation. Envision yourself in a Viennese coffee shop, the lovely decor filled with the calm murmur of customers enjoying their coffee and cakes.

When entering a coffee shop, it is usual to welcome the workers and say "Bitte" (please) when ordering. Austrians value courtesy, and little acts of kindness go a long way. Take your time savoring your coffee, possibly with a slice of Sachertorte, and engage yourself in the atmosphere.

Dress Code

Austrians dress conservatively and neatly for work, social gatherings, or casual outings. Envision walking through Vienna's city center and seeing individuals dressed smartly, reflecting the country's appreciation for elegance and decorum. Wear a smart casual or professional dress to blend in at a formal function or a great restaurant.

Punctuality

Punctuality is highly prized in Austria, and arriving on time is interpreted as a sign of respect and dependability. If you're seeing a friend for coffee or attending a business meeting, try to arrive a few minutes early. Envision your host's delight when you arrive on time, ready to participate in the planned activity without delay.

Social Etiquette

Austrians are often reserved but friendly once they get to know you. It's critical to be respectful and considerate in your dealings. Avoid bringing up sensitive themes like politics or personal economics in casual interactions. Instead, have chats about culture, travel, and common interests. Consider starting a conversation with a native about the beauty of the Austrian Alps or the charm of the country's medieval villages.

When visiting someone's home, it is usual to take off your shoes at the door and wear the slippers provided by the host. This modest gesture demonstrates respect for the home and the host's efforts to prepare for your visit.

Celebrations and Traditions

Austria has many traditions, and attending local events can be fun to learn about the country. Consider partaking in the celebratory atmosphere of Fasching (Carnival), where people dress up in spectacular costumes and attend parades and parties. Envision yourself at a traditional Almabtrieb festival in the autumn, when decorated cattle are driven down from the alpine meadows surrounded by music, dancing, and feasting.

Understanding and respecting Austrian etiquette and customs will improve your trip experience and allow you to connect more deeply with the locals and their way of life. By embracing these traditions, you will be greeted with open arms and leave with lasting memories of visiting this wonderful country.

TRAVEL CHECKLIST

Essential Documents

Passport

First and foremost, you will require a valid passport. Ensure your passport is current and will not expire within six months of your intended travel date. Envision the thrill of getting your passport stamped as you enter Austria, eager to see everything it has to offer. It's always a good idea to make a couple of photocopies of your passport—keep one with you, separate from your original, and leave another with a trusted friend or family member at home.

Visa

Depending on your nationality, you may require a visa to visit Austria. However, you do not need a visa to enter Austria if you are from the EU or a Schengen Area country. If you are not from one of these regions, check the exact visa requirements well before your travel. Consider the relief of having your visa arranged and ready, giving you piece of mind as you begin your Austrian trip.

Many people can enter Austria on a Schengen visa for short periods (up to 90 days within 180 days). Apply for a visa at your home country's Austrian embassy or consulate. Gather proof of housing, travel insurance, and sufficient finances for your stay ahead of time, as the application procedure may demand these.

Travel Insurance

While not necessarily required, travel insurance is strongly advised for any trip overseas. Austria's healthcare system is good, but travel insurance can protect you from unforeseen medical bills. Consider the peace of mind that comes with knowing you're protected against medical crises, vacation cancellations, and misplaced luggage. When selecting a travel insurance plan, ensure that it covers health, accidents, and any activities you intend to engage in, such as skiing or hiking.

Health Documentation

Although Austria does not have special vaccine requirements for visitors, it is prudent to have your standard vaccinations up to date. Consider the comfort of knowing you're completely prepared, with all relevant health papers on hand.

Accommodation Confirmation

When traveling, having paper or digital copies of your hotel reservations is helpful. These confirmations are useful at customs and immigration and provide peace of mind knowing where you'll spend each night. Envision effortlessly checking into your quaint Austrian hotel or snug Airbnb, ready to begin your tour without a hitch.

Transportation Documents

If traveling to Austria by aircraft, rail, or car, arranging your transit documentation is critical. Keep your flight tickets and boarding credentials easily accessible. A Eurail pass or individual train tickets may be required if you're traveling by train. You'll need an international driving permit (IDP) and a valid driver's license if you want to drive. Envision how easy it would be to navigate Austrian roads and trains knowing you have all of the essential documents.

Financial Documents

Ensure you have enough money for your vacation. While credit and debit cards are generally accepted in Austria, bringing cash for minor purchases or in isolated places is advisable. Notify your bank of your travel plans to avoid card complications while overseas. Consider the simplicity of being able to pay for your wonderful Wiener Schnitzel or a slice of Sachertorte without difficulty.

Emergency Contacts

Make a list of emergency contacts, including the local embassy or consulate, your lodging, and a few trusted individuals from home. Keep this list handy, if on your phone or written out. Consider the security of having all your critical numbers at your fingertips, just in case you need them.

Personal Identification

Bring another form of identification, such as a driver's license or an ID card, in addition to your passport. Some establishments may require supplementary identification for specific services, which can be useful. Consider the convenience of being able to instantly display your ID when required.

Itinerary

Finally, preserve a copy of your trip itinerary, which includes airline information, lodging addresses, and planned activities. This not only keeps you organized but also allows your family and friends back home to know where you are. Envision the convenience of having your entire journey planned and accessible at a glance.

Packing Tips

The weather in Austria varies greatly based on the season and place you visit. Check the forecast for your trip dates and pack accordingly. Envision trekking in the Alps in the summer or touring Christmas markets in the winter; your wardrobe should be appropriate for the season.

Layers are essential, especially if you're traveling in the spring or fall when the weather might be unpredictable. Consider lightweight, breathable layers for daytime warmth and an additional layer for cooler evenings.

Select apparel that can be mixed and matched to create multiple outfits. Neutral hues and basic pieces are ideal for this. Consider how much easier it would be to get ready daily if your wardrobe was organized and versatile.

Comfortable footwear is essential if you're touring city streets or trekking trails. Bring a pair of solid walking shoes or sneakers, and if you intend to dine out or attend events, pack dressier footwear.

To save space, bring travel-sized toiletries. Remember that many items can be acquired at your destination if necessary. Consider passing through airport security with your small toiletries bag.

Bring a modest daypack for day trips. It's ideal for carrying essentials like a wallet, water bottle, and light jacket. Envision yourself comfortably carrying everything you need for a day of sightseeing.

Keep your important paperwork (passport, visa, travel insurance, etc.) in a safe, easily accessible area. A travel document organizer can be really useful.

What to Pack

Clothing

- Tops
- Bottoms
- Outerwear
- Layers
- Sleepwear
- Undergarments
- Winter accessories

Footwear

- Walking Shoes
- Dress Shoes
- Sandals

Toiletries

- Basic Toiletries
- Skincare
- Hair Care
- Medications

Travel Essentials

- Documents
- Money
- Electronics
- Entertainment
- Reusable Water Bottle
- Snacks

Extras

- Umbrella
- Travel Pillow
- Notebook and Pen

Travel Insurance

Travel insurance is your safety net, protecting against unforeseen incidents that may impair your trip. Consider this: you've booked your flights, reserved a lovely hotel in Vienna, and meticulously planned every aspect of your journey. But then, out of nowhere, an unexpected illness, misplaced luggage, or airline cancellation threatens to derail everything. This is where travel insurance comes in, covering expenses and offering aid when needed.

Types of Coverage

There are various types of travel insurance, each designed to cover different aspects of your journey:

Trip Cancellation and Interruption: This covers the costs of canceling your trip due to unforeseen situations such as illness, family emergencies, or extreme weather. Envision having peace of mind knowing that your financial investment is safe even if something unexpected happens.

Medical Insurance: This is essential when going overseas and covers medical bills if you become ill or injured. Envision hiking in the breathtaking Austrian Alps and suddenly needing medical assistance. Travel insurance ensures you receive essential care without worrying about high medical expenditures.

Baggage and Personal Belongings : Missing or delayed luggage can greatly inconvenience you. This coverage compensates you for lost or damaged luggage and personal possessions. Envision landing in Austria only to discover that your luggage did not make the trip. With insurance, you can immediately replace necessary items and continue your travel.

Emergency Evacuation: If you ever need emergency medical evacuation, this coverage can save you a lot of money. Consider visiting isolated areas of Austria; if something goes wrong, you'll have access to rapid and professional emergency services.

Travel Delay: If your flight is delayed, this coverage will reimburse you for extra expenses like lodging and meals. Consider a lengthy layover turning into an overnight delay. Travel insurance can help cover unforeseen expenses while keeping your budget intact.

24/7 support Services: Most travel insurance policies include access to support services, which cover everything from medical emergencies to lost passports. Envision you're in a strange place and desperate need of aid. Having a dedicated support line can mean the difference.

Choosing the Right Plan

Choosing the proper travel insurance requires considering your specific needs and vacation plans. Here are some tips to help you:

Consider the length of your trip, the activities you plan to perform, and the location. For example, if you plan to ski in the Austrian Alps, ensure your policy includes adventurous sports.

Compare the plans various insurance companies offer. Pay attention to coverage limitations, exclusions, and the fine print. A policy with comprehensive coverage may cost more, but it will provide better protection.

Some credit cards include travel insurance as a perk. Examine what's included and decide if more coverage is needed.

In the big scheme of things, travel insurance is a small expense that can significantly impact. It enables you to confidently explore, knowing that you're covered whatever happens.

WHEN TO VISIT

Best Time of Year

Spring (March-May):

Springtime in Austria is a season of regeneration and brilliant colors. As the snow melts and flowers grow, the environment transforms into a fairytale setting. Envision wandering through Vienna's Stadtpark, where the trees are budding, and the air is filled with the scent of new blossoms.

Spring is the best time to visit if you prefer milder weather and fewer crowds. The temperatures are pleasant, ranging from 10°C to 20°C (50°F to 68°F). It's ideal for touring cities, climbing in the Alps, or attending the many cultural events and festivals that begin to emerge.

Personal Tip: *Pack layers! The weather is erratic, with cool mornings and evenings but scorching afternoons. Don't forget an umbrella; April showers are typical.*

Summer (June–August):

Summer is the major tourist season in Austria and with good reason. The weather is pleasant, with average temperatures ranging from 20°C to 30°C (68°F to 86°F). The days are long, so you have plenty of time to explore the outdoors and soak up the sun.

This is the season for festivals. Envision attending the world-famous Salzburg Festival, where the streets are bustling with music, opera, and theater acts. Envision hiking in the Austrian Alps, surrounded by beautiful green meadows and wildflowers in bloom.

However, plan for greater crowds and higher prices. Tourists flock to popular places such as Vienna, Salzburg, and Innsbruck.

Personal Tip: *Make reservations and purchase tickets for popular attractions well in advance. If you want to hike, start early in the morning to escape the heat and crowds.*

Autumn (September–November):

Autumn in Austria is just magical. The landscapes are painted in gold, orange, and red to reflect the changing colors of the leaves. The temperatures are milder, ranging from 10°C to 20°C (50°F to 68°F), making it an ideal time to explore.

Harvest festivals and wine-tasting events are in full swing, providing a sample of Austria's culinary offerings. Envision strolling through a Wachau Valley vineyard, enjoying freshly pressed grape juice and local wines.

The mobs drop out after the summer, allowing for a more calm experience. It's also an ideal time for outdoor activities such as hiking, motorcycling, and exploring the gorgeous villages.

Personal Tip: *Bring a nice camera to photograph the beautiful fall leaves. Dress in layers because mornings and evenings might be cool, but afternoons are usually mild.*

Winter (December–February):

If you enjoy winter activities, Austria is a dream come true. The Alps are snow-covered, providing some of Europe's best skiing and snowboarding. Envision sliding down the slopes of St. Anton or Kitzbühel while surrounded by stunning mountain landscapes.

Winter is also the season for Christmas markets, which decorate cities and towns with dazzling lights and festive decorations. Envision yourself strolling through Vienna's Christkindlmarkt, sipping hot mulled wine, and visiting stalls selling handmade crafts and delectable delicacies.

Although the temperatures can be fairly chilly, frequently dropping below zero, the allure and beauty of winter make it worthwhile. Simply cuddle up and appreciate the season.

Personal Tip: *Invest in quality winter clothing, including warm coats, gloves, caps, and waterproof boots. Consider hiring a small alpine cabin for an authentic Austrian winter experience.*

Seasonal Highlights

Spring (March-May):

Blooming Gardens and Parks

Spring brings new life to Austria's gardens and parks. Envision walking through Schönbrunn Palace Gardens in Vienna or Mirabell Gardens in Salzburg, where colorful flowers and lush greenery offer a lovely environment ideal for a leisurely walk or picnic.

Easter markets

In Austria, Easter is celebrated with bright marketplaces full of artistically painted eggs, traditional crafts, and delectable food. Envision yourself meandering around these delightful markets, trying local sweets like Osterpinze, and enjoying the joyful ambiance.

Outdoor activities

As the weather warms, it's the perfect time for outdoor activities. Hiking trails in areas such as the Salzkammergut and Tyrol begin to emerge, providing spectacular vistas of the blooming landscape. Cycling in the Wachau Valley, with its picturesque vineyards and riverbank trails, is another springtime treat.

Festivals & Events

Spring also signals the beginning of different cultural festivals. For example, the Styriarte Festival in Graz honors classical music with performances inspired by the region's history and customs. Envision going to an open-air concert surrounded by the beauty of spring.

Summer (June to August):

Music and Art Festivals

Summer is the busiest season for festivals in Austria. The world-renowned Salzburg Festival floods the city with opera, plays, and concerts. Envision yourself enjoying a performance amid Salzburg's ancient settings, where the beauty of music is in the air.

Alpine adventures

The Alps serve as a playground for outdoor enthusiasts during the summer. Hiking, mountain biking, and climbing are all popular hobbies. Envision hiking in the Zillertal Alps, with breathtaking views of snow-capped peaks and green valleys.

Lake activities

Austria's lakes, including Wolfgangsee and Lake Neusiedl, are ideal for swimming, sailing, and kayaking. Envision relaxing by the crystal-clear waters, soaking up the sun, and admiring the tranquil beauty of these alpine lakes.

Vienna Open-Air Cinema

Vienna's Rathausplatz Film Festival hosts open-air screenings of operas, concerts, and films, resulting in a vibrant cultural scene. Envision a balmy summer evening spent witnessing a famous performance under the stars against the stunning backdrop of Vienna City Hall.

Autumn (September–November):

Autumn foliage

In October, the Austrian countryside becomes a canvas of golden and scarlet hues. Consider driving through the Wachau Valley or the Vienna Woods, where the fall colors create a breathtaking, quiet environment.

Wine Harvest & Festivals

Autumn is the harvest season in Austria's wine regions. Sturmzeit (young wine season) is commemorated with wine festivals and tastings. Envision yourself in a charming village, surrounded by vineyards, savoring fresh wine and local specialties.

Cultural events

A variety of cultural activities take place during the autumn season. The Vienna Worldwide Film Festival features worldwide films, attracting moviegoers from all around the world. Envision immersing yourself in the realm of film through screenings and discussions that honor cinematic brilliance.

Outdoor Exploration

The cooler temperatures make it ideal for trekking and exploring. The Hohe Tauern National Park provides excellent autumn hiking with fewer visitors. Envision yourself on a picturesque walk, breathing in the fresh air and taking in the breathtaking views.

Winter (December–February):

Christmas markets

Winter in Austria is renowned for enchanting Christmas markets. Consider going to the Christkindlmarkt in Vienna, where you can enjoy hot mulled wine, gingerbread, and handmade goods in a joyful setting. The markets in Salzburg and Innsbruck are similarly fascinating, providing a true winter wonderland atmosphere.

Skiing & Snowboarding

The Austrian Alps are a winter sports enthusiast's paradise. Consider skiing down the slopes of St. Anton, Kitzbühel, or Zell am See, with immaculate snow and well-maintained paths. The après-ski culture, which includes snug mountain huts selling warm drinks and hearty meals, adds to the appeal.

New Year's Eve Celebrations

Austrians celebrate New Year's Eve, also known as Silvester, with huge events. Vienna hosts the Vienna Philharmonic's New Year's Concert, broadcast worldwide. Consider the excitement and energy as the city comes alive with fireworks, parties, and joyful celebrations.

Winter Hiking & Snowshoeing

For a quieter winter experience, consider winter trekking or snowshoeing in Tyrol or the Salzkammergut. Consider traveling across snowy regions, where the solitude of winter produces a serene, almost magical environment.

Thermal spas

Winter is also an ideal season to unwind at Austria's thermal spas. Envision relaxing in warm, mineral-rich waters in places like Längenfeld's Aqua Dome or Rogner Bad Blumau, surrounded by snowy surroundings.

GETTING THERE

By Air

Major Airports

Austria is well-connected to the world through several international airports, each offering modern facilities and a range of services.

Vienna International Airport (VIE)

Located just 18 kilometers southeast of Vienna, this is Austria's largest and busiest airport. It serves as a major hub for international flights and is well-connected to cities across Europe, North America, Asia, and beyond. Picture arriving at a sleek, modern airport with easy access to the city center.

Salzburg Airport (SZG)

Situated about 4 kilometers from Salzburg's city center, this airport is perfect if you're heading to the scenic region of Salzburg and the nearby Alpine resorts. It's smaller than Vienna's airport but offers a charming and efficient entry point to Austria.

Innsbruck Airport (INN)

Nestled in the heart of the Alps, Innsbruck Airport is ideal for those visiting Tyrol and its famous ski resorts. Envision landing amidst stunning mountain scenery, ready to hit the slopes or explore the picturesque towns.

Graz Airport (GRZ)

Located 9 kilometers south of Graz, this airport serves the southeastern part of Austria. It's a convenient entry point for exploring the cultural and historical treasures of Graz and the surrounding region.

Practical Tips for a Smooth Journey

Booking Your Flight

Start by comparing flights on popular travel websites like Skyscanner, Expedia, or Kayak. Look for direct flights if possible, as they save time and reduce the hassle of layovers. For the best deals, book your tickets well in advance, especially if you're traveling during peak seasons like summer or the winter holidays.

Travel Documents

- Ensure your passport is valid for at least six months beyond your planned departure date. Depending on your nationality, you might need a visa to enter Austria. Check the Austrian embassy or consulate website in your country for specific requirements. For many travelers from the US, Canada, and the EU, a visa isn't required for short stays.

Airport Transfers

From Vienna International Airport, you can easily reach the city center by train, bus, or taxi. The City Airport Train (CAT) is a quick and comfortable option, taking just 16 minutes to get to Vienna's central station. Alternatively, the S-Bahn (suburban railway) is a more budget-friendly choice. Envision a smooth and scenic ride into the heart of Vienna, ready to start your adventure.

Salzburg and Innsbruck airports offer convenient shuttle services and public transport options to their respective city centers. For Graz, you can take a train or bus from the airport to the city, making it easy to start exploring right away.

Arrival and Customs

Upon arrival, follow the signs for customs and immigration. Have your passport, boarding pass, and any required documents ready. The process is usually quick and straightforward, but be prepared for occasional questions about your stay.

Contact Information

It's always good to have contact details for your airline and the airport handy. Here are some useful contacts:

- Vienna International Airport: +43 1 70070
- Salzburg Airport: +43 662 85800
- Innsbruck Airport: +43 512 22525
- Graz Airport: +43 316 29020

Personal Recommendations

If you have a layover, Vienna International Airport offers a range of amenities to make your wait comfortable. There are excellent dining options, duty-free shops, and even a wellness area where you can relax. Envision enjoying a delicious meal or a quick spa session before your next flight.

For those traveling during the winter sports season, Innsbruck Airport has services catering to skiers and snowboarders, including special luggage handling for your gear. Picture the convenience of having your equipment ready to go as soon as you land.

If you're traveling with family, look for airports with family-friendly facilities. Vienna and Salzburg airports have play areas and child-friendly services, ensuring a stress-free experience for parents and kids alike.

By Train

From Germany

Austria shares a robust rail network with Germany, making it one of the easiest and most popular ways to travel. High-speed trains like ICE (InterCity Express) and Railjet connect major German cities such as

Munich, Frankfurt, and Berlin with Austrian cities like Vienna, Salzburg, and Innsbruck. Picture yourself gliding through picturesque landscapes, with the rolling hills and charming villages of Bavaria giving way to the stunning Austrian Alps.

From Switzerland

Traveling from Switzerland to Austria by train is equally scenic and convenient. The Railjet service connects Zurich with Vienna, offering a direct route that takes about 8 hours. Envision crossing the Swiss Alps, with breathtaking views of snow-capped peaks and crystal-clear lakes, making the journey itself a memorable part of your trip.

From Italy

If you're coming from Italy, the ÖBB Nightjet and Railjet trains provide excellent connections between cities like Venice, Milan, and Rome to Vienna and other Austrian destinations. Envision boarding a comfortable night train in Venice, falling asleep to the gentle rocking of the carriage, and waking up in the heart of Vienna, ready to explore the city's imperial charm.

From Hungary

Hungary's capital, Budapest, is just a few hours away from Vienna by train, making it a popular and convenient route. The Railjet service connects these two cities in about 2.5 hours. Picture yourself enjoying the scenic ride along the Danube River, with rolling hills and historic towns passing by your window.

Practical Tips for a Smooth Journey

Booking Your Tickets

It's best to book your train tickets in advance, especially during peak travel seasons. Websites like the ÖBB (Austrian Federal Railways), DB (Deutsche Bahn) and Rail Europe offer easy online booking options.

Early booking often comes with discounts, so keep an eye out for special deals.

Seat Reservations

While not always mandatory, seat reservations are highly recommended, particularly on popular routes and high-speed trains. This ensures you have a comfortable seat, especially during busy travel times. Envision having a reserved window seat, perfect for taking in the scenic views along the way.

Arrival and Transfers

Most international trains to Austria will stop at major stations such as Vienna Hauptbahnhof (Hbf), Salzburg Hbf, or Innsbruck Hbf. These stations are well-connected to local public transportation, making it easy to reach your final destination. Picture stepping off the train and seamlessly transitioning to a tram or bus that takes you straight to your hotel or first sightseeing stop.

Border Controls

While Austria is part of the Schengen Area, which allows for passport-free travel between member countries, it's always good to have your passport or ID handy. Occasionally, there may be spot checks, so keeping your documents accessible ensures a smooth journey.

Onboard Services

High-speed and international trains in Europe often come equipped with amenities like Wi-Fi, dining cars, and power outlets. Envision enjoying a delicious meal or a cup of coffee in the dining car while watching the stunning scenery pass by.

Contact Information

Having contact details for the railway companies can be helpful in case of any issues or questions during your journey. Here are some useful contacts:

- ÖBB (Austrian Federal Railways): +43 5 1717
- DB (Deutsche Bahn): +49 30 2970
- SBB (Swiss Federal Railways): +41 51 220 11 11
- Trenitalia: +39 06 68475475

Personal Recommendations

If you have the time, opt for scenic routes that take you through beautiful landscapes. The route from Zurich to Vienna via the Arlberg Pass offers some of the most spectacular views in the Alps. Envision taking in the dramatic mountain scenery and picturesque valleys, making your journey as memorable as the destination.

For longer journeys, consider taking a night train like the ÖBB Nightjet. This allows you to save on accommodation costs and arrive refreshed in the morning. Picture yourself in a cozy sleeper cabin, drifting off to sleep and waking up in a new city, ready to explore.

By Car

From Germany

Austria shares an extensive and well-maintained road network with Germany, making it one of the most convenient routes. The A8 Autobahn from Munich to Salzburg is a popular choice, offering a scenic drive through the Bavarian countryside before crossing into Austria. Picture cruising along the highway, with the Alps gradually coming into view, signaling the start of your Austrian adventure.

From Switzerland

Driving from Switzerland to Austria is equally picturesque. The A1 Autobahn from Zurich to Innsbruck takes you through stunning alpine landscapes, with plenty of opportunities for scenic stops. Envision winding through mountain passes, with panoramic views of snow-capped peaks and lush valleys.

From Italy

If you're starting in Italy, the A22 Autobahn from Verona to Innsbruck is a fantastic route, taking you through the breathtaking Brenner Pass. Picture driving through the heart of the Alps, with towering mountains on either side and charming alpine villages dotting the landscape.

From Hungary

The M1 motorway from Budapest to Vienna is a direct and efficient route, offering a smooth drive through the Hungarian plains and into Austria. Envision the excitement of crossing the border and seeing the sign welcoming you to Austria, with Vienna's cultural and historical treasures just a short drive away.

Practical Tips for a Smooth Journey

Planning Your Route

Use reliable GPS or navigation apps like Google Maps or Waze to plan your route and get real-time traffic updates. Consider alternative routes to avoid congestion and make the most of your drive. Envision having a well-planned journey, with scenic detours and interesting stops along the way.

Toll Roads and Vignettes

Austria has a well-maintained network of toll roads and highways. To drive on these roads, you'll need to purchase a vignette, a toll sticker that must be displayed on your windshield. Vignettes can be bought at border crossings, gas stations, or online. Picture yourself breezing through the highways, knowing you've got all the necessary permits.

Vehicle Requirements

Ensure your car is in good condition before embarking on your trip. Check the tires, brakes, and fluid levels, and make sure you have a spare tire, jack, and basic tools. It's also mandatory to carry a reflective vest, warning triangle, and first-aid kit in your car. Envision the peace of mind knowing your vehicle is well-prepared for the journey.

Driving Regulations

Familiarize yourself with Austrian driving laws and regulations. The speed limits are generally 130 km/h on highways, 100 km/h on rural roads, and 50 km/h in urban areas. Austria also has strict laws against drinking and driving, with a blood alcohol limit of 0.5 mg/ml. Picture yourself driving responsibly and safely, enjoying the beautiful Austrian scenery.

Parking

Parking in Austrian cities can be challenging, especially in popular tourist destinations. Look for designated parking garages or park-and-ride facilities on the outskirts of cities like Vienna and Salzburg. Picture yourself parking hassle-free and using public transport to explore the city center.

Border Controls

While Austria is part of the Schengen Area, which allows for passport-free travel between member countries, it's always good to have your passport or ID handy. Occasionally, there may be spot checks, so keeping your documents accessible ensures a smooth journey.

Contact Information

It's always good to have contact details for roadside assistance and local services handy. Here are some useful contacts:

- ÖAMTC (Austrian Automobile Club): +43 1 71199
- ARBÖ (Austrian Automobile, Motorcycle and Touring Club): +43 1 123

Personal Recommendations

Make the journey part of your adventure by planning scenic stops along the way. If you're driving from Munich to Salzburg, take a detour to visit the beautiful Chiemsee Lake. If you're coming from Italy, stop in the charming town of Vipiteno. Envision these little breaks adding delightful surprises to your road trip.

Take advantage of roadside eateries and local restaurants to sample regional cuisine. Picture yourself enjoying a hearty Austrian meal at a cozy Gasthaus (inn) in a small village, savoring local specialties like Wiener Schnitzel and apple strudel.

One of the joys of a road trip is the flexibility it offers. Don't hesitate to take spontaneous detours or extend your stay in a particularly charming location. Envision the freedom to explore off-the-beaten-path destinations and create unique memories.

Austria has numerous fuel stations along major routes, so refueling is easy. However, in more remote areas, it's wise to fill up your tank whenever you have the chance. Picture yourself driving confidently, knowing you're well-prepared for the journey.

GETTING AROUND

Public Transportation

Trains

Austria's train network, operated by ÖBB (Austrian Federal Railways), is extensive and reliable, connecting cities, towns, and rural areas. High-speed trains like Railjet provide fast connections between major cities such as Vienna, Salzburg, Innsbruck, and Graz, while regional trains cover shorter distances and smaller towns.

High-Speed Trains (Railjet)

Railjet trains are equipped with comfortable seating, free Wi-Fi, dining services, and power outlets. A one-way ticket from Vienna to Salzburg starts at around €25 if booked in advance.

Regional Trains

Regional trains offer frequent services and connect many destinations. A regional train ticket from Vienna to Melk, for instance, costs approximately €16.

Tickets can be purchased at train stations, online via the ÖBB website (www.oebb.at), or through the ÖBB mobile app. The ÖBB Vorteilscard offers discounts of up to 50% on train tickets and costs €66 per year.

Buses

Buses complement the train network, reaching destinations that might not have rail service. Companies like FlixBus and PostBus provide extensive coverage.

Intercity and Regional Buses

FlixBus offers connections between major cities and towns, with fares starting as low as €5. PostBus covers regional routes, making it ideal for exploring rural areas.

Local Buses

Local bus services in cities like Vienna, Salzburg, and Graz are frequent and reliable. Tickets are typically €2.40 for a single ride in Vienna.

Tickets for local buses can be bought at kiosks, ticket machines, or directly from the driver. Day passes and multi-day passes are available and offer unlimited travel within the city.

Trams

Trams are a popular mode of transport in Austrian cities, providing an efficient and scenic way to travel.

Vienna's Tram Network

Vienna boasts one of the world's largest tram networks, with routes covering most parts of the city. A single ticket costs €2.40, while a 24-hour ticket is €8.

Other Cities

Graz, Linz, and Innsbruck also have extensive tram networks. A single tram ride in Graz costs €2.50.

Tram tickets can be bought at machines, kiosks, or via mobile apps. Integrated tickets for trams, buses, and trains simplify travel plans.

Subways and Metros

Vienna is the only Austrian city with a full-fledged metro system, known as the U-Bahn. It's fast, efficient, and covers all major areas of the city.

Vienna U-Bahn

The U-Bahn has five lines (U1 to U6) and runs frequently. A single ticket costs €2.40, and a 72-hour pass is €17.10.

Tickets can be bought at stations, online, or via the Wiener Linien app. Options include single tickets, day passes, and weekly passes.

Driving in Austria

Driving in Austria offers the freedom to explore the country's stunning landscapes and charming towns at your own pace. From the majestic Alps to historic cities, a road trip in Austria can be an unforgettable experience.

Requirements for Driving in Austria

Driving License

Visitors from EU/EEA countries can use their domestic driving licenses in Austria. Travelers from non-EU/EEA countries should carry an International Driving Permit (IDP) along with their domestic license.

Age Requirements

The minimum age for driving a car in Austria is 18 years. For renting a car, most rental companies require drivers to be at least 21 years old and have held a license for a minimum of one year. Some companies may charge an additional fee for drivers under 25.

Vehicle Documentation

Ensure you carry your driving license, vehicle registration documents, and proof of insurance at all times while driving.

Road Rules and Regulations

Speed Limits

- Motorways (Autobahn): 130 km/h (81 mph)
- Rural Roads: 100 km/h (62 mph)
- Urban Areas: 50 km/h (31 mph)
- Residential Zones: 30 km/h (19 mph)

Seat Belts

Seat belts are mandatory for all passengers. Fines apply for non-compliance.

Alcohol Limits

The legal blood alcohol limit is 0.5 mg/ml. For drivers who have held their license for less than two years, the limit is 0.1 mg/ml. Austria has strict penalties for driving under the influence.

Toll Roads and Vignettes

To use Austria's motorways, you need to purchase a vignette (toll sticker). Vignettes can be bought at border crossings, gas stations, or online. Prices are approximately €9.90 for 10 days, €29 for two months, and €96.40 for a year. Display the vignette on your windshield to avoid fines.

Winter Tires

From November 1 to April 15, winter tires are mandatory. In snowy conditions, snow chains may also be required, particularly in mountainous areas.

Parking

In cities, look for blue zones (short-term parking areas), where you can park for a limited time with a parking disc. Parking garages and park-and-ride facilities are also available. Always check local parking regulations to avoid fines.

Navigating the Roads

Signage

Austrian road signs follow international conventions and are generally easy to understand. Familiarize yourself with key signs before your trip.

Fuel Stations

Fuel stations are plentiful and often include amenities such as restaurants and shops. Major credit cards are widely accepted. In rural areas, it's wise to fill up whenever you have the chance.

Road Conditions

Austrian roads are well-maintained, but be prepared for winding mountain routes, especially in the Alps. Drive cautiously and be aware of weather conditions, which can change rapidly.

Emergency Numbers

In case of emergency, dial 112 for general emergencies or 122 for fire services, 133 for police, and 144 for ambulance services.

Renting a Car

Major car rental companies such as Avis, Hertz, Europcar, and Sixt operate throughout Austria. Book your rental car in advance, especially during peak travel seasons.

Basic insurance is usually included in car rental agreements, but consider additional coverage for peace of mind. Collision damage waiver (CDW) and theft protection are recommended.

You can rent a car at airports, major train stations, and city centers. Verify the pickup and drop-off procedures with your rental company to ensure a smooth experience.

Scenic Drives and Routes

Grossglockner High Alpine Road

This famous route offers breathtaking views of Austria's highest peak, the Grossglockner. The road winds through the Hohe Tauern National Park, providing stunning vistas and numerous lookout points.

The Romantic Road

This picturesque route takes you through charming medieval towns and beautiful landscapes. Highlights include the towns of Krems, Melk, and the Wachau Valley, a UNESCO World Heritage site known for its vineyards and historic architecture.

The Styrian Wine Road

Explore the scenic wine country of Styria, with its rolling hills and quaint villages. Stop at local wineries for tastings and enjoy the region's culinary delights.

Innsbruck to Bregenz

Drive through the heart of the Alps along this stunning route. Highlights include the vibrant city of Innsbruck, the historic town of Feldkirch, and the beautiful Lake Constance.

Cycling and Walking

Austria is a cyclist's dream, with a vast network of well-marked bike paths that cater to all levels of fitness and experience. One of the most popular routes is the Danube Cycle Path (Donauradweg), which stretches from Passau in Germany to Vienna. This scenic route follows the course of the Danube River, passing through picturesque villages, lush vineyards, and historic castles. As you pedal along, you'll be treated to breathtaking views and plenty of opportunities to stop and explore.

For those seeking more of a challenge, the Austrian Alps offer thrilling mountain biking trails with varying degrees of difficulty. The region around Innsbruck, for example, boasts a wide range of trails that take you through forests, over mountain passes, and along ridges with panoramic views. Envision the rush of descending a winding alpine trail, the crisp mountain air filling your lungs, and the stunning scenery stretching out before you.

Bike rentals are widely available in cities and tourist areas, making it easy to hop on a bike and start your adventure. Many rental shops also offer electric bikes (e-bikes), which can be a great option for tackling hilly terrain without breaking a sweat. If you're an avid cyclist or just looking for a leisurely ride, Austria's diverse cycling routes cater to all preferences.

Walking and Hiking

Walking and hiking in Austria is equally rewarding, offering an up-close and personal experience of the country's natural beauty. The well-marked hiking trails range from gentle strolls through meadows and forests to challenging alpine climbs. One of the most famous hiking routes is the Eagle Walk (Adlerweg) in Tyrol, which spans over 400 kilometers and offers breathtaking views of the Alps. Each section of the trail reveals new landscapes, from tranquil valleys to rugged peaks, making every step an adventure.

If you prefer urban exploration, Austria's cities are perfect for walking tours. Vienna, with its grand architecture and rich history, is a walker's paradise. Stroll along the Ringstraße, a circular boulevard that encircles the historic city center, and marvel at landmarks like the State Opera House, Hofburg Palace, and the Parliament Building. Salzburg, the birthplace of Mozart, offers charming cobblestone streets, beautiful gardens, and historic sites such as Hohensalzburg Fortress and Mirabell Palace.

The Austrian countryside is dotted with quaint villages and serene landscapes that are best explored on foot. The Wachau Valley, a UNESCO World Heritage site, is renowned for its picturesque vineyards and medieval castles. Walking trails in this region meander through vineyards, along the Danube River, and past charming villages like Dürnstein and Spitz. Take your time to sample local wines, enjoy a leisurely meal at a traditional Heuriger (wine tavern), and soak in the serene beauty of the valley.

Practical Tips

When planning a cycling or walking trip in Austria, consider the following tips to make your experience as enjoyable as possible. First, always check the weather forecast and dress appropriately. Layered clothing is ideal, as it allows you to adjust to changing temperatures and conditions. Comfortable shoes are essential for both walking and cycling, and don't forget sunscreen and a hat for sun protection.

For longer hikes or bike rides, carry a map or use a GPS device to stay on track. Many trails are well-marked, but having a navigation tool can provide extra peace of mind. It's also wise to pack a small first-aid kit, water, and snacks to keep you energized throughout your journey.

If you're renting a bike, make sure it's in good condition and properly adjusted to your size. Helmets are highly recommended for safety, especially on mountain biking trails. Some rental shops offer guided tours, which can be a great way to explore new areas with the expertise of a local guide.

VIENNA: THE IMPERIAL CITY

Vienna, the capital of Austria, is a city that effortlessly blends imperial grandeur with modern sophistication. Known for its rich history, stunning architecture, and vibrant cultural scene, Vienna is a destination that captivates visitors from the moment they arrive.

Vienna's history dates back to Roman times, but it truly flourished during the Habsburg Empire, when it became a center of power, art, and culture. The city's historic core, a UNESCO World Heritage site, is a testament to its imperial past. Walking through the Innere Stadt (Inner City), you'll encounter grand boulevards, elegant squares, and architectural marvels at every turn.

One of the most iconic landmarks is the Hofburg Palace, the former imperial residence of the Habsburgs. Today, it houses several museums, including the Imperial Apartments, the Sisi Museum, and the Austrian National Library. Nearby, the stunning St. Stephen's Cathedral, with its striking Gothic architecture and colorful tiled roof, stands as a symbol of Vienna's enduring legacy.

Vienna is synonymous with music, having been home to some of the world's greatest composers, including Mozart, Beethoven, and Strauss. The city's musical heritage is celebrated in its numerous concert halls and opera houses. The Vienna State Opera, one of the leading opera houses globally, offers outstanding performances throughout the year. Attending an opera or a concert in Vienna is an experience not to be missed.

The city is also a treasure trove for art lovers. The Kunsthistorisches Museum houses one of the most significant art collections in the world, featuring works by artists such as Bruegel, Raphael, and Vermeer. The Belvedere Palace, another must-visit, showcases an impressive collection of Austrian art, including Gustav Klimt's famous painting "The Kiss."

While Vienna honors its past, it is also a vibrant, modern city. The MuseumsQuartier, one of the largest cultural complexes in the world, is a hub for contemporary art and culture. Here, you can explore museums like the Leopold Museum, dedicated to Austrian modern art, and the mumok, which focuses on modern and contemporary art.

Vienna's food scene is equally diverse, offering everything from traditional Viennese cuisine to innovative international dishes. No visit to Vienna is complete without trying a Wiener Schnitzel, a classic Austrian dish. And, of course, the city's coffee houses are legendary. Places like Café Central and Café Sacher provide the perfect setting to enjoy a cup of coffee and a slice of Sachertorte, a decadent chocolate cake.

Vienna is also known for its beautiful parks and green spaces, offering a refreshing contrast to its urban environment. The Prater, with its iconic giant Ferris wheel, is a vast public park that's perfect for a leisurely stroll or a bike ride. The Schönbrunn Palace gardens, another UNESCO World Heritage site, are a stunning example of Baroque landscape design and offer panoramic views of the city.

The Danube Island, a long narrow island in the middle of the Danube River, is a popular recreational area with beaches, walking trails, and numerous outdoor activities. If you're looking to relax or engage in some active pursuits, Vienna's green spaces provide plenty of options.

Vienna is well-connected and easy to navigate. The city's public transportation system, including trams, buses, and the U-Bahn (subway), is efficient and user-friendly. Day passes and multi-day tickets are available, offering unlimited travel on all forms of public transport.

For travelers, Vienna International Airport provides convenient access to the city, with direct connections to major destinations around the world. From the airport, the City Airport Train (CAT) and the S-Bahn provide quick and easy transportation to the city center.

Must-See Attractions

Schönbrunn Palace

First on our list is the magnificent Schönbrunn Palace. This former summer residence of the Habsburgs is a stunning example of Baroque architecture and a UNESCO World Heritage site. Wandering through its opulent rooms, you'll get a glimpse into the lives of Austria's imperial family.

Key Highlights

The Grand Tour of the palace includes 40 rooms, featuring the lavish Great Gallery and the exquisite Hall of Mirrors.

Don't miss the beautiful gardens, especially the Gloriette, which offers a panoramic view of Vienna.

Practical Information

- Location: Schönbrunner Schloßstraße 47, 1130 Vienna
- Opening Hours: Daily from 8:00 AM to 5:30 PM (hours vary seasonally)
- Ticket Prices: Grand Tour: €22.00 (adults), €14.50 (children)

St. Stephen's Cathedral

St. Stephen's Cathedral, or Stephansdom, is the heart of Vienna and a symbol of the city. This Gothic masterpiece, with its striking multicolored tile roof, dominates the skyline and offers a fascinating glimpse into Vienna's medieval past.

Key Highlights

Climb the South Tower for a breathtaking view of the city.

Explore the catacombs and the impressive Pummerin bell in the North Tower.

Admire the intricate details of the High Altar and the beautifully carved pulpit.

Practical Information

- Location: Stephansplatz 3, 1010 Vienna
- Opening Hours: Monday to Saturday from 6:00 AM to 10:00 PM, Sunday from 7:00 AM to 10:00 PM
- Ticket Prices: South Tower: €5.50 (adults), €2.00 (children)

Hofburg Palace

The Hofburg Palace, the former imperial palace of the Habsburg dynasty, is now home to several museums and the official residence of the President of Austria. This sprawling complex is a treasure trove of history and art.

Key Highlights

Visit the Imperial Apartments, where you can see the lavish rooms of Emperor Franz Joseph and Empress Elisabeth (Sisi).

Explore the Sisi Museum, dedicated to the life and legacy of the beloved empress.

Don't miss the Austrian National Library and the stunning State Hall.

Practical Information

- Location: Michaelerkuppel, 1010 Vienna
- Opening Hours: Daily from 9:00 AM to 5:30 PM
- Ticket Prices: Combined ticket for Imperial Apartments, Sisi Museum, and Silver Collection: €15.00 (adults), €9.00 (children)

Belvedere Palace

The Belvedere is actually two palaces – the Upper and Lower Belvedere – set in a beautiful Baroque park. It's famous for housing an impressive collection of Austrian art, including works by Gustav Klimt.

Key Highlights

The Upper Belvedere's highlight is Klimt's masterpiece, "The Kiss," alongside other works by Schiele and Kokoschka.

The Lower Belvedere showcases medieval and Baroque art and architecture.

Practical Information

- Location: Prinz Eugen-Straße 27, 1030 Vienna
- Opening Hours: Daily from 10:00 AM to 6:00 PM
- Ticket Prices: Upper Belvedere: €16.00 (adults), €13.50 (students and seniors)

Vienna State Opera

A visit to Vienna wouldn't be complete without experiencing its world-famous music scene. The Vienna State Opera is one of the leading opera houses globally, with a history of exceptional performances.

Key Highlights

Attend an opera or ballet performance; the repertoire is extensive and world-class.

Take a guided tour to learn about the history and architecture of this iconic building.

Practical Information

- Location: Opernring 2, 1010 Vienna

- Opening Hours: Box office hours: Monday to Friday from 9:00 AM to 8:00 PM; tours are typically available daily
- Ticket Prices: Performance tickets vary widely; tours cost around €9.00 (adults), €4.00 (children)

Naschmarkt

For a taste of local life, head to the Naschmarkt, Vienna's most famous market. This bustling market has been a culinary hotspot since the 16th century, offering a vibrant mix of fresh produce, international foods, and local delicacies.

Key Highlights

Sample a variety of foods, from Viennese pastries to exotic spices and cheeses.

Enjoy a meal at one of the many small restaurants and food stalls, offering everything from traditional Austrian dishes to international cuisine.

Practical Information

- Location: Wienzeile, 1060 Vienna
- Opening Hours: Monday to Friday from 6:00 AM to 7:30 PM, Saturday from 6:00 AM to 6:00 PM (closed on Sundays)

Prater and the Giant Ferris Wheel

The Prater is a large public park in Vienna, home to the iconic Giant Ferris Wheel (Riesenrad), one of the city's most recognizable landmarks. It's a great place for families and those looking for a bit of fun and relaxation.

Key Highlights

Ride the Giant Ferris Wheel for panoramic views of Vienna.

Explore the amusement park with its rides and attractions, suitable for all ages.

Enjoy a leisurely walk or a picnic in the extensive green spaces.

Practical Information

- Location: Prater, 1020 Vienna
- Opening Hours: The park is open 24/7; the Ferris Wheel operates daily from 10:00 AM to 9:45 PM (hours vary seasonally)
- Ticket Prices: Ferris Wheel: €12.00 (adults), €5.00 (children)

Best Areas to Stay

Innere Stadt (First District)

If it's your first visit and you want to be in the heart of the action, stay in the Innere Stadt.

The Innere Stadt is Vienna's historic center and offers an unparalleled experience of the city's imperial grandeur and cultural richness. Here, you're surrounded by iconic landmarks like St. Stephen's Cathedral, the Hofburg Palace, and the Vienna State Opera. The district's charm lies in its blend of medieval alleyways, elegant boulevards, and grand squares. Staying here means you can walk to most major attractions, making it incredibly convenient.

Crowd Level: High. The Innere Stadt is always bustling with tourists, especially around popular sights and shopping streets. However, its central location and historical significance make it worth the crowds.

You'll be engaged in Vienna's history and culture, with easy access to the city's top attractions, dining, and shopping. It's ideal for first-time visitors and those who want to be at the center of Vienna's vibrant city life.

Leopoldstadt (Second District)

For a balanced mix of green spaces and urban excitement, choose Leopoldstadt.

Leopoldstadt, just across the Danube Canal from the city center, offers a unique mix of nature and city life. The Prater, a large public park with the iconic Giant Ferris Wheel, is perfect for outdoor activities and leisurely strolls. The district's multicultural atmosphere is reflected in its diverse shops, cafes, and restaurants.

Crowd Level: Moderate. While the Prater attracts many visitors, the residential areas are quieter, providing a more relaxed environment compared to the Innere Stadt.

You get the best of both worlds – proximity to the city center and access to extensive green spaces. It's great for families and those who enjoy a blend of outdoor activities and urban convenience.

Neubau (Seventh District)

If you love art, culture, and a trendy atmosphere, stay in Neubau.

Neubau is Vienna's creative hub, known for its vibrant art scene, independent boutiques, and lively nightlife. The MuseumsQuartier, a massive cultural complex, is the highlight of this district, offering contemporary art, design, and performance spaces. The district's youthful energy and eclectic vibe attract artists, students, and young professionals.

Crowd Level: Moderate to High. The MuseumsQuartier and popular nightlife spots can be busy, especially in the evenings and weekends. However, the area maintains a laid-back, bohemian feel.

Neubau is perfect for those who appreciate modern culture and creativity. It's an excellent choice for art lovers, fashion enthusiasts, and anyone looking to experience Vienna's contemporary side.

Wieden (Fourth District)

For a blend of history, culture, and a bohemian atmosphere, Wieden is a great choice.

Wieden is a charming district that offers a relaxed, bohemian vibe with historical elegance. The Belvedere Palace, with its stunning gardens and art collections, is a major draw. The Naschmarkt, Vienna's largest market, adds a lively and colorful touch to the district, offering a variety of foods and goods.

Crowd Level: Moderate. While popular spots like the Naschmarkt can be busy, the overall atmosphere is more laid-back compared to the city center.

Wieden provides a mix of cultural attractions and a relaxed environment. It's ideal for foodies, history buffs, and those looking to stay slightly off the main tourist trail while still being close to key attractions.

Landstraße (Third District)

For a quieter, more residential stay with cultural highlights, consider Landstraße.

Landstraße offers a diverse, centrally located neighborhood with cultural landmarks and green spaces. The district is home to the Hundertwasserhaus, a unique architectural gem, and the MAK – Museum of Applied Arts. The Stadtpark, with its serene atmosphere and famous statues, is perfect for relaxation.

Crowd Level: Low to Moderate. Landstraße is generally quieter and less touristy than the Innere Stadt, offering a more residential feel.

Landstraße is great for travelers who prefer a quieter, more local experience while still being close to the city center. It's perfect for those who enjoy cultural sites and peaceful parks.

Shopping in Vienna

Kärntner Straße and Graben

Let's start with the heart of Vienna's shopping scene, Kärntner Straße and Graben. These are the main pedestrian shopping streets in the Innere Stadt (the first district), and they're packed with a mix of luxury brands, international stores, and charming cafes.

What to Expect

High-End Boutiques: You'll find luxury brands like Louis Vuitton, Gucci, and Chanel here, perfect if you're in the mood for some high-end shopping.

International Chains: Stores like H&M, Zara, and Mango are also scattered along these streets, offering trendy fashion at more affordable prices.

Mariahilfer Straße

If you're looking for a more extensive shopping experience, head to Mariahilfer Straße, Vienna's longest and most popular shopping street. It stretches from the city center to Westbahnhof and is lined with a diverse range of stores.

What to Expect

Fashion Chains: You'll find all the big names here, from H&M and Forever 21 to Desigual and Foot Locker.

Department Stores: Don't miss Peek & Cloppenburg for a wide selection of fashion brands under one roof.

Local Boutiques: Explore side streets and alleys for unique Austrian boutiques offering something a bit different.

Naschmarkt

For a different kind of shopping experience, Naschmarkt is a must-visit. This vibrant market is not only a food lover's paradise but also a great place to pick up unique items.

What to Expect

Fresh Produce and Specialty Foods: The market is filled with stalls selling fresh fruits, vegetables, spices, cheeses, and meats. It's the perfect place to sample local delicacies.

Antiques and Flea Market: On Saturdays, there's a flea market at the Naschmarkt where you can find everything from vintage clothing and jewelry to antiques and curiosities.

Kohlmarkt and Goldenes Quartier

For those who love luxury shopping, Kohlmarkt and the Goldenes Quartier are where you'll want to be. This area, also located in the Innere Stadt, is home to some of the most prestigious brands in the world.

What to Expect

Luxury Brands: Stores like Cartier, Tiffany & Co., and Valentino are just a few of the high-end names you'll find here.

Elegant Atmosphere: The architecture and ambiance are as luxurious as the shopping, making it a pleasure to stroll through.

Brunnenmarkt and Yppenplatz

If you're looking for a more local and authentic experience, Brunnenmarkt and the nearby Yppenplatz in the 16th district are fantastic. This area offers a multicultural vibe and a great mix of products.

What to Expect

Local Produce and Foods: The market is known for its fresh produce, meats, and spices, reflecting the area's diverse population.

Handmade Goods: You can also find unique handmade items, from clothing and accessories to home decor.

Nightlife and Entertainment

Vienna's nightlife is unique because it blends the city's rich cultural heritage with a modern, cosmopolitan vibe. Envision starting your evening with a sophisticated cocktail in a grand baroque setting, moving on to a vibrant club with cutting-edge electronic music, and ending the night at a cozy heuriger (wine tavern) sipping on local wines. The city's nightlife is as varied as its history, offering a perfect mix of elegance, energy, and authenticity.

Popular Nightlife Areas

Bermuda Triangle (Bermudadreieck)

This is one of Vienna's most famous nightlife districts, located in the Innere Stadt. The Bermuda Triangle is packed with bars, pubs, and clubs, making it the perfect place to bar-hop and experience different vibes all in one night.

Lively and diverse, with a mix of locals and tourists. You'll find everything from quiet pubs to bustling dance floors.

Most venues open around 6 PM and stay open until 4 or 5 AM. Entry fees vary, but many bars have free entry, while clubs might charge €5-€15.

Gürtel

The Gürtel is an area along Vienna's outer ring road, famous for its vibrant club scene. Many of the clubs here are housed under old railway arches, giving them a unique and edgy atmosphere.

Trendy and energetic, popular with a younger crowd and those who love live music and DJ sets.

Clubs typically open around 10 PM and stay open until the early hours of the morning. Entry fees range from €5-€20, depending on the event and the venue.

Naschmarkt and Kettenbrückengasse

This area is perfect for those who prefer a more relaxed and hip atmosphere. The Naschmarkt, known for its food market during the day, transforms into a lively nightlife spot in the evening, with a variety of bars and eateries.

Hip and laid-back, with a mix of young professionals and creatives. Great for enjoying craft cocktails and good conversation.

Bars and restaurants here usually open around 5 PM and close by 2 AM. Entry is generally free.

Donaukanal

The Donaukanal area is a popular summer spot with numerous bars, beach clubs, and floating venues along the canal. It's a fantastic place to enjoy warm evenings with great drinks and scenic views.

Casual and chill, perfect for those who enjoy an outdoor vibe and riverside views. The crowd is a mix of locals and visitors.

Venues along the Donaukanal typically open from early afternoon until midnight or later. Entry is usually free.

Must-Visit Venues

Loos American Bar

Designed by the famous architect Adolf Loos, this bar is an iconic spot in Vienna. It's known for its classic cocktails and elegant, intimate setting. Open daily from 12 PM to 4 AM. Cocktails are around €10-€15. No entry fee, but seating is limited, so arrive early.

Volksgarten

One of Vienna's oldest and most famous clubs, Volksgarten combines a beautiful garden setting with an indoor dance floor. It's a hotspot for both locals and tourists. Open Thursday to Saturday from 11 PM to 6 AM. Entry fees range from €10-€20, depending on the event.

Pratersauna

Located near the Prater amusement park, Pratersauna is a club with a unique history and vibe. It features multiple dance floors, an outdoor pool, and a sauna, creating a fun and eclectic atmosphere. Open Fridays and Saturdays from 11 PM to 6 AM. Entry fees range from €10-€15.

Flex

Known for its underground music scene, Flex is a legendary club on the Donaukanal that hosts live concerts and DJ sets, focusing on electronic, indie, and alternative music. Open from Wednesday to Saturday, 11 PM to 6 AM. Entry fees vary from €5-€15.

Exploring Vienna

Innere Stadt

Start your journey in the Innere Stadt, Vienna's historic core and a UNESCO World Heritage site. This area is a treasure trove of architectural marvels and historical landmarks. Begin at St. Stephen's Cathedral, an iconic Gothic masterpiece with a striking multicolored tile roof. Climb the South Tower for panoramic views of the city. Just a short walk away is the Hofburg Palace, the former imperial residence. Here, you can explore the Imperial Apartments, the Sisi Museum, and the Austrian National Library. Don't miss the Spanish Riding School, where you can watch the world-famous Lipizzaner horses perform.

Neubau

For a taste of Vienna's modern and creative side, head to Neubau. This trendy neighborhood is home to the MuseumsQuartier, one of the largest cultural complexes in the world. The area boasts contemporary art museums, design shops, and cool cafes. The Leopold Museum and mumok (Museum of Modern Art) are must-visits for art enthusiasts. Neubau's streets are lined with independent boutiques, vintage shops, and stylish bars, making it a perfect place for a leisurely stroll and some shopping.

Prater and Leopoldstadt

Escape the urban hustle and bustle with a visit to the Prater in Leopoldstadt. The Prater is a large public park known for its iconic Giant Ferris Wheel, which offers fantastic views over Vienna. The park itself is perfect for a leisurely bike ride or a picnic. Nearby, the Augarten is another beautiful park with impressive baroque gardens and the famous porcelain factory, Augarten Porzellanmanufaktur.

Leopoldstadt is also home to a vibrant multicultural community, adding a rich diversity to the area's atmosphere and cuisine.

The Ringstraße

The Ringstraße, or Ring Road, encircles the Innere Stadt and is lined with some of Vienna's most important and opulent buildings. Take a leisurely tram ride or walk along the Ringstraße to admire the stunning architecture. Key highlights include the Vienna State Opera, the Kunsthistorisches Museum, the Naturhistorisches Museum, and the Austrian Parliament Building. This grand boulevard also features lush parks like the Burggarten and the Volksgarten, where you can take a break from sightseeing and enjoy a peaceful moment in the city's green spaces.

Naschmarkt and Kettenbrückengasse

For a true taste of local life, visit the Naschmarkt, Vienna's most famous market. Located near Kettenbrückengasse, the Naschmarkt is a bustling hub of activity with a variety of stalls selling fresh produce, spices, cheeses, meats, and ready-to-eat dishes from around the world. It's a great place to sample local delicacies like Wiener Schnitzel, Käsekrainer (cheese-filled sausages), and various pastries. On Saturdays, the adjacent flea market offers a treasure trove of antiques, vintage clothes, and curiosities.

Schönbrunn Palace and Gardens

A trip to Vienna wouldn't be complete without visiting Schönbrunn Palace, the former summer residence of the Habsburgs. This baroque masterpiece, located a bit outside the city center, is surrounded by beautifully manicured gardens, fountains, and even a zoo. The Grand Tour of the palace takes you through the opulent state rooms and private apartments. After exploring the interior, spend some time wandering the extensive gardens and climb up to the Gloriette for a panoramic view of Vienna.

Spittelberg and Beyond

For a charming and slightly off-the-beaten-path experience, head to Spittelberg, a quaint neighborhood known for its narrow streets and historic buildings. This area is particularly enchanting during the Christmas season, when it hosts one of Vienna's most picturesque Christmas markets. The cobblestone streets are lined with small shops, art galleries, and cozy restaurants. It's a wonderful place to explore if you enjoy a more intimate, village-like atmosphere within the city.

SALZBURG: THE CITY OF MOZART

Historical Sites and Museums

Hohensalzburg Fortress

First up, we have the iconic Hohensalzburg Fortress, one of the largest and best-preserved medieval castles in Europe. Perched atop Festungsberg hill, it offers stunning panoramic views of Salzburg and the surrounding Alps.

Key Exhibits and Collections

The Fortress Museum: Showcases historical artifacts, including medieval weaponry, historical documents, and exhibits on the daily life of the castle's inhabitants.

The Marionette Museum: Features a charming collection of marionettes and the history of puppet theater in Salzburg.

The State Rooms: These opulent rooms reflect the grandeur of the prince-archbishops who once resided here.

Practical Information

- Opening Hours: Daily from 9:30 AM to 5:00 PM (extended hours in summer).
- Ticket Prices: Standard adult tickets are €12.90, with discounts for children, students, and seniors. Combination tickets for the fortress and funicular are available.

Mozart's Birthplace (Mozart Geburtshaus)

No visit to Salzburg would be complete without paying homage to Wolfgang Amadeus Mozart. His birthplace, located in the heart of the Old Town, is now a museum dedicated to the life and work of the musical genius.

Key Exhibits and Collections

Mozart's Early Years: Explore the rooms where Mozart was born and lived during his early years, filled with personal items, portraits, and original instruments.

Original Manuscripts: The museum houses a significant collection of Mozart's original compositions and letters.

Interactive Exhibits: Learn about Mozart's life and music through interactive displays and multimedia installations.

Practical Information

- Opening Hours: Daily from 9:00 AM to 5:30 PM (extended hours in summer).
- Ticket Prices: Adult tickets are €12.00, with reduced rates for children, students, and seniors.

Salzburg Museum

Located in the Neue Residenz, the Salzburg Museum offers a comprehensive overview of the city's history, art, and culture. It's an excellent place to start your exploration of Salzburg's rich heritage.

Key Exhibits and Collections

Permanent Collection: Includes artifacts from prehistoric times to the present, showcasing Salzburg's cultural and historical evolution.

Art Gallery: Features works by local and international artists, with a focus on the baroque period.

Interactive Displays: Engage with multimedia exhibits that bring Salzburg's history to life.

Practical Information

- Opening Hours: Tuesday to Sunday from 9:00 AM to 5:00 PM (closed on Mondays).
- Ticket Prices: Adult tickets are €9.00, with discounts for children, students, and seniors. Combination tickets for the Salzburg Museum and Panorama Museum are available.

DomQuartier

The DomQuartier offers a unique tour through the interconnected buildings of the Salzburg Cathedral, the Residenz, and St. Peter's Abbey. This historic complex provides a fascinating glimpse into the religious and political life of Salzburg's past.

Key Exhibits and Collections

Cathedral Museum: Displays sacred art, liturgical objects, and relics from the cathedral's treasury.

State Rooms: The opulent rooms of the Residenz, where the prince-archbishops held court and conducted state business.

Long Gallery: A stunning baroque gallery featuring portraits of Salzburg's rulers and important figures.

Practical Information

- Opening Hours: Wednesday to Monday from 10:00 AM to 5:00 PM (closed on Tuesdays).
- Ticket Prices: Adult tickets are €13.00, with discounts for children, students, and seniors. Combination tickets for multiple attractions are available.

Hellbrunn Palace and Trick Fountains

A short distance from the city center, Hellbrunn Palace is famous for its whimsical trick fountains and beautiful gardens. This baroque palace was the summer residence of the Salzburg prince-archbishops.

Key Exhibits and Collections

Trick Fountains: The highlight of Hellbrunn, these playful water features are designed to surprise and delight visitors with unexpected sprays and jets of water.

Palace Rooms: Explore the opulent rooms and learn about the history of the palace and its residents.

Folk Museum: Located in the nearby Monatsschlössl, this museum showcases traditional Austrian folk art and culture.

Practical Information

- Opening Hours: April to November, daily from 9:00 AM to 4:30 PM (extended hours in summer).
- Ticket Prices: Adult tickets are €13.50, with reduced rates for children, students, and seniors. Tickets include entry to the palace and trick fountains.

Special Events and Programs

Salzburg is renowned for its cultural events and festivals, which often include special programs at its museums and historical sites. The Salzburg Festival, held every summer, is one of the world's most prestigious music and drama festivals, featuring performances in stunning historical settings. During Advent, the city comes alive with charming Christmas markets, special exhibitions, and festive events.

Salzburg's Music Scene

First off, you can't talk about Salzburg's music scene without mentioning Mozart. Born in 1756, Mozart is one of the most influential composers in Western music history, and his legacy is deeply woven into the fabric of the city. A visit to Mozart's Birthplace (Mozart Geburtshaus) in the Getreidegasse is a must. The museum there offers fascinating insights into his early life, with original manuscripts, instruments, and family portraits.

After that, head over to Mozart's Residence (Mozart Wohnhaus) on Makartplatz. This museum showcases his life in Salzburg and his extensive body of work. These visits are not just educational; they're a chance to feel a personal connection with the musical genius who once walked these streets.

Salzburg Festival

One of the highlights of Salzburg's music calendar is the Salzburg Festival, held every summer. This world-renowned festival, founded in 1920, is a spectacular celebration of opera, drama, and classical music. Picture yourself sitting in the Großes Festspielhaus, the grand festival hall, listening to top-tier performances by internationally acclaimed artists. The festival's setting in various historic venues around the city adds an extra layer of magic to the experience.

Mirabell Palace and Gardens

For a more casual yet equally enchanting musical experience, the Mirabell Palace and its stunning Baroque gardens host frequent concerts. The Marble Hall (Marmorsaal) in the palace is one of the most beautiful wedding halls in the world and serves as an intimate venue for chamber music concerts. Envision listening to a live string quartet while surrounded by ornate marble and gold decor.

Mozarteum University

The Mozarteum University, named after the city's famous son, is a prestigious music and performing arts university. It regularly hosts public concerts, recitals, and masterclasses featuring both students and renowned guest artists. These performances offer a chance to see emerging talent and enjoy high-quality music in a more relaxed, academic setting.

Traditional Folk Music

Don't leave Salzburg without experiencing some traditional Austrian folk music. Head to a local heuriger (wine tavern) or beer garden where you can enjoy live performances of folk music, complete with accordions, zithers, and yodeling. Places like the Stiegl-Brauwelt or the Augustiner Bräu Mülln offer a fantastic combination of hearty Austrian cuisine, local beers, and lively music.

Hidden Gems and Local Venues

Beyond the famous sites, Salzburg is dotted with smaller venues and hidden gems that offer incredible musical experiences. The Jazzit Music Club, for example, is a hot spot for jazz lovers, featuring local and international artists in an intimate setting. For something a bit different, the ARGEkultur offers a diverse program of contemporary music, theater, and performance art.

Where to Stay

Altstadt (Old Town)

Stay in Altstadt if you want to be in the heart of Salzburg's historical and cultural attractions.

The Altstadt, or Old Town, is Salzburg's historic center and a UNESCO World Heritage site. It's characterized by its narrow cobblestone streets, baroque architecture, and iconic landmarks such as the Salzburg Cathedral, Hohensalzburg Fortress, and Mozart's Birthplace. This area is perfect for those who want to engage themselves in the city's rich history and culture. Staying here means you'll be within walking distance of major attractions, museums, and charming squares like Residenzplatz and Kapitelplatz.

Crowd Level: High. The Old Town is popular with tourists year-round, particularly in the summer and during the Christmas season.

Altstadt is ideal for first-time visitors and history enthusiasts who want to be in the midst of Salzburg's most iconic sights and vibrant cultural scene.

Neustadt (New Town)

Choose Neustadt for a blend of historical charm and modern amenities, just across the river from the Old Town.

Neustadt, or the New Town, is located on the opposite bank of the Salzach River from the Old Town. It offers a mix of historical buildings and modern conveniences, providing a slightly quieter alternative to the bustling Altstadt. Neustadt is home to the beautiful Mirabell Palace and Gardens, as well as the Mozarteum University of Salzburg.

Crowd Level: Moderate. Neustadt is less crowded than the Old Town but still lively, especially around Mirabell Palace and during cultural events.

Neustadt is perfect for travelers who want to be close to the Old Town while enjoying a quieter, more relaxed atmosphere with easy access to green spaces and cultural venues.

Nonntal

Stay in Nonntal for a peaceful, residential neighborhood with easy access to both the city center and nature.

Nonntal is a tranquil district located south of the Old Town, offering a more residential feel with beautiful views of the surrounding hills. It's a great choice for those who prefer a quieter stay while still being within walking distance of the city's main attractions. The area is home to the historic Nonnberg Abbey, the oldest continuously inhabited nunnery in the German-speaking world.

Crowd Level: Low. Nonntal is a quieter, more residential area with fewer tourists.

Nonntal is ideal for those seeking a peaceful retreat with easy access to both the city center and natural attractions. It's perfect for families and travelers looking for a more authentic local experience.

Maxglan

Choose Maxglan for a mix of modern amenities and traditional charm, with excellent transport links.

Maxglan is a district located west of the Old Town, known for its blend of modern and traditional elements. The area offers a variety of shops, cafes, and restaurants, along with beautiful residential streets and parks. Maxglan is also conveniently located near Salzburg Airport, making it a great choice for travelers with early or late flights.

Crowd Level: Moderate. Maxglan is a residential area with a steady flow of locals and visitors, but it's less touristy than the city center.

Maxglan is perfect for travelers who want a convenient location with good transport links, modern amenities, and a touch of traditional Austrian charm.

Outdoor Activities

Hiking and Walking

Salzburg is surrounded by breathtaking alpine landscapes, making it a hiker's dream. If you're a seasoned hiker or just looking for a leisurely walk, there are trails to suit all levels.

Practical Tips

For beginners, the Gaisberg Loop offers stunning views without being too challenging. More experienced hikers might enjoy the Untersberg, which offers panoramic vistas from its summit. Spring through autumn are ideal for hiking, as the weather is generally pleasant and the trails are clear.

Equipment: Sturdy hiking boots, a backpack with water and snacks, and a map or GPS device. Don't forget a hat and sunscreen for those sunny days.

Personal Recommendations

Gaisberg: Easily accessible from the city, Gaisberg offers several trails with varying difficulty levels. The views of Salzburg from the top are simply breathtaking.

Lake Fuschlsee: For a more leisurely walk, the path around Lake Fuschlsee is perfect. It's a 12-kilometer trail with picturesque views of the crystal-clear lake.

Cycling

Salzburg is incredibly bike-friendly, with numerous well-maintained paths that take you through the city, along the river, and into the surrounding countryside. It's a fantastic way to explore more of what Salzburg has to offer at your own pace.

Practical Tips

You can easily rent bikes from various shops around the city. Consider renting an e-bike if you plan to tackle more hilly terrain.

Always wear a helmet and follow local cycling rules. Salzburg's paths are well-marked, but it's good to have a map or GPS.

Equipment: A bike, helmet, comfortable clothing, and a water bottle. Some bike rental shops also provide panniers if you plan to carry a picnic or extra gear.

Personal Recommendations

Tauern Cycle Path: This scenic route follows the Salzach River and offers stunning views of the Alps and charming villages along the way.

Hellbrunn Alley: A flat and easy route that takes you to Hellbrunn Palace. The tree-lined path is beautiful, and the palace grounds are perfect for a picnic.

Kayaking and Canoeing

Paddling down the Salzach River gives you a unique perspective of Salzburg's beautiful landscape. It's an exciting and refreshing way to explore the area, especially in the warmer months.

Practical Tips

For beginners, booking a guided tour is a great way to get started. Experienced guides will provide all necessary equipment and ensure your safety. Make sure to go on a day with good weather and calm water conditions for the best experience.

Equipment: Life jacket, paddle, waterproof clothing, and a dry bag for your belongings. Most tours include equipment rental.

Personal Recommendations

Salzach River Tour: Join a guided tour that starts from the city and paddles downstream. It's suitable for all levels and provides fantastic views of the city and surrounding countryside.

Lake Wolfgangsee: For a more tranquil experience, kayaking on Lake Wolfgangsee is idyllic. The clear waters and stunning alpine backdrop make it a paddler's paradise.

Paragliding

Envision soaring above the Austrian Alps, taking in panoramic views of Salzburg's breathtaking landscapes. Paragliding offers an exhilarating way to see the region from a whole new perspective.

Practical Tips

Paragliding experiences are popular, so it's a good idea to book in advance. Many operators offer tandem flights with experienced pilots. Dress in layers, as it can be cooler at higher altitudes. Sturdy shoes and a windproof jacket are essential.

Equipment: The paragliding company will provide all necessary equipment, including harnesses and helmets.

Personal Recommendations

Gaisberg: This is one of the best spots for paragliding near Salzburg. The views over the city and surrounding mountains are unbeatable.

Werfenweng: Another fantastic location, Werfenweng offers a variety of flight paths with stunning alpine scenery.

Skiing and Snowboarding

In the winter months, Salzburg transforms into a snowy wonderland, making it a prime destination for skiing and snowboarding. The nearby Alps offer world-class slopes for all skill levels.

Practical Tips

Resorts like Obertauern, Flachau, and Zell am See are all within easy reach of Salzburg and offer a range of slopes and facilities. Most ski resorts have rental shops where you can get skis, snowboards, boots, and helmets. Always follow the ski resort's safety guidelines and stay within marked trails.

Personal Recommendations

Obertauern: Known for its reliable snow conditions and extensive slopes, Obertauern is perfect for both beginners and experienced skiers.

Flachau: A family-friendly resort with excellent facilities and a variety of slopes. It's also part of the larger Ski Amadé network, offering access to multiple resorts.

Exploring Salzburg

Altstadt (Old Town)

The heart of Salzburg is its Altstadt, or Old Town, a UNESCO World Heritage site brimming with baroque architecture, cobblestone streets, and historical landmarks. As you wander through the narrow lanes, you'll encounter the majestic Salzburg Cathedral, a masterpiece of baroque art and architecture. Nearby, the Residenz Palace offers a glimpse into the opulent lifestyle of the prince-archbishops, with its lavish state rooms and art galleries. Don't miss the iconic Hohensalzburg Fortress, perched high above the city. This fortress not only offers panoramic views but also houses museums and historical exhibits.

Getreidegasse and Mozart's Birthplace

One of the most famous streets in Salzburg is Getreidegasse, known for its charming wrought-iron shop signs and historical buildings. This bustling street is also home to Mozart's Birthplace (Mozart Geburtshaus), where the musical genius was born in 1756. The museum inside offers fascinating insights into Mozart's early life and his prolific career, featuring original instruments, portraits, and family memorabilia.

Mirabell Palace and Gardens

Cross the Salzach River to the New Town (Neustadt) and you'll find the exquisite Mirabell Palace and Gardens. The palace itself, built in the early 17th century, is famous for its Marble Hall, a venue for concerts and weddings. The gardens are a visual delight, with beautifully manicured lawns, fountains, and sculptures. The Pegasus Fountain and the Dwarf Garden are particularly charming and perfect for a leisurely stroll.

Hellbrunn Palace and Trick Fountains

A short drive from the city center takes you to Hellbrunn Palace, a baroque villa built in the early 17th century by Prince-Archbishop Markus Sittikus. The palace is renowned for its trick fountains, designed to surprise and amuse guests with hidden water jets and playful mechanisms. The expansive grounds also feature beautiful gardens and a serene park, perfect for a relaxed afternoon.

Leopoldskron Palace

For fans of "The Sound of Music," a visit to Leopoldskron Palace is a must. This picturesque palace, located on the outskirts of Salzburg, was used as the von Trapp family home in the iconic film. While the palace itself is a private venue, you can walk around the beautiful grounds and enjoy the stunning views of the lake and the surrounding mountains.

Auer Welsbach Park and the Augustiner Bräu

For a more local experience, head to Auer Welsbach Park, a lovely green space perfect for a leisurely walk or a picnic. Adjacent to the park is the Augustiner Bräu, a historic brewery founded by monks in 1621. This traditional beer hall offers a genuine taste of Austrian beer culture, with large communal tables and a bustling, friendly atmosphere. Grab a stein of their delicious beer and some hearty Austrian fare from the food stalls.

Kapuzinerberg

For those who enjoy hiking and breathtaking views, Kapuzinerberg offers a perfect escape from the city's hustle and bustle. This small mountain located in the heart of Salzburg provides several walking trails, leading to panoramic viewpoints and the Capuchin Monastery. The paths are well-marked and suitable for all fitness levels, offering a peaceful retreat with stunning vistas of the city and the surrounding Alps.

INNSBRUCK: THE HEART OF THE ALPS

Ski Resorts and Winter Sports

Innsbruck, often referred to as the "Capital of the Alps," is a haven for ski enthusiasts. Nestled amidst towering peaks, the city offers easy access to several world-class ski resorts, each with its own unique appeal. If you're a seasoned skier or a first-time snow adventurer, Innsbruck's ski resorts are sure to offer something for everyone.

Nordkette - Urban Skiing with a View

Just a stone's throw from the city center, Nordkette is a favorite for skiers who want to blend a city getaway with alpine thrills. The Nordkette cable car, known for its striking design, transports skiers from Innsbruck's vibrant heart to the slopes in just 20 minutes. You can enjoy breathtaking views of the city and the snow-capped mountains as you race down the slopes.

- Best for: Fast access to ski slopes and stunning views of the city and mountains.
- Terrain: Varied, with some challenging runs for advanced skiers.
- Highlight: The breathtaking views of Innsbruck from the top of the resort.

Stubai Glacier - Snow Sure All Year Round

A true winter paradise, the Stubai Glacier is one of the largest ski resorts in Austria, offering skiing well into the summer months. It is perfect for both beginners and experts, with a wide range of slopes and excellent snow reliability. The glacier's high altitude ensures fantastic conditions from October through June.

- Best for: Snow-sure conditions and a long ski season.

- Terrain: A mix of beginner, intermediate, and advanced slopes.
- Highlight: Skiing with the backdrop of the majestic glacier, and access to cross-country skiing trails.

Axamer Lizum - A Ski Resort for Families

Located just 19 kilometers from Innsbruck, Axamer Lizum is a great choice for families and intermediate skiers. The resort offers a variety of slopes that are suitable for all levels, along with a friendly atmosphere. With 40 kilometers of well-maintained slopes, it's an excellent option for those seeking a more relaxed but still thrilling experience.

- Best for: Family-friendly skiing and relaxed slopes.
- Terrain: Mostly intermediate-level runs, some advanced options.
- Highlight: Excellent off-piste and powder skiing areas for more adventurous skiers.

Kühtai - The High-Altitude Ski Resort

At 2,020 meters above sea level, Kühtai is Austria's highest ski resort. Thanks to its lofty position, it offers excellent snow conditions and a wide variety of runs. Kühtai is a bit more off the beaten path compared to the other resorts, providing a more tranquil skiing experience with fewer crowds.

- Best for: High-altitude skiing with excellent snow conditions.
- Terrain: A good mix of runs for all skill levels.
- Highlight: Stunning mountain panoramas and top-tier snow conditions.

Winter Sports in Innsbruck

Innsbruck is not just for skiers; it is a haven for a wide variety of winter sports, from traditional alpine activities to newer, adrenaline-pumping options. The surrounding mountains and picturesque villages host activities that will keep you on your toes throughout the entire winter season.

Skiing and Snowboarding

Skiing and snowboarding remain the star attractions, and Innsbruck caters to all types of skiers. If you're looking for groomed, fast slopes or untouched powder for backcountry adventures, you'll find it all. The city itself offers great access to all the major resorts, making it a central point for snow sports enthusiasts.

Tip: If you're a beginner, don't miss out on the ski schools that cater to all ages and skill levels in resorts like Axamer Lizum and Kühtai.

Tobogganing

If you want to experience the joy of speeding down a snowy slope but in a slightly less technical way, tobogganing is a fun option. Innsbruck offers several toboggan runs, including the Glungezer Toboggan Run, which stretches over 3.5 kilometers and provides plenty of thrills as it winds down through the mountains.

Tip: Some runs are floodlit in the evening, making for an exciting nighttime toboggan experience.

Ice Climbing

For those seeking a true winter adventure, ice climbing is a must-try in the Innsbruck region. The towering cliffs and frozen waterfalls around the city offer the perfect setting for this exhilarating sport. Beginners can take guided tours with experienced climbers, while experts can challenge themselves on the more technical ice formations.

- Best for: Experienced climbers or those wanting to try something unique.

- Location: The Stubai Valley is home to several fantastic ice climbing spots.

Winter Hiking and Snowshoeing

For those who prefer a slower pace, winter hiking and snowshoeing offer a fantastic way to explore the winter landscape at a more relaxed tempo. Innsbruck boasts numerous well-maintained trails that are ideal for winter hiking, with scenic routes leading through snowy forests and past alpine meadows. Snowshoeing is particularly popular in the Sellrain Valley and the Stubai Alps, offering opportunities for serene escapes into the mountains.

Tip: Guided tours are available to help you discover the hidden beauty of the region.

Ice Skating and Curling

Innsbruck has several rinks where visitors can enjoy a leisurely session of ice skating. One of the most popular places to skate is the OlympiaWorld, an indoor arena used during the 1964 and 1976 Winter Olympics. For something a bit more traditional, try your hand at curling, a quintessential winter sport enjoyed by locals in the region.

Cross-Country Skiing

The Innsbruck region offers over 150 kilometers of cross-country skiing trails, catering to both classic and skate skiing. The trails are situated in idyllic locations, including the Stubai Valley, where you can glide past scenic villages and pristine forests. Cross-country skiing is perfect for those looking to explore the landscape at a more leisurely pace.

Summer Activities

Innsbruck is surrounded by dramatic mountain ranges, making it one of the top destinations for hiking in Europe. The region offers trails for all levels, from easy walks to challenging mountain climbs, each providing stunning views and the chance to explore the pristine alpine wilderness.

Nordkette – A Hiker's Dream

Just a short distance from the city center, Nordkette is a hiker's paradise, offering trails that vary in difficulty. The Hafelekar Peak provides panoramic views of Innsbruck and the surrounding valleys. For a relaxing walk, you can follow trails that wind through alpine meadows, while more experienced hikers can ascend to the summit for a greater challenge.

- Cost: A return ticket for the Nordkette Cable Car to Hafelekar Peak costs around €30 per person. Hiking itself is free.

Stubai Valley – The Long Distance Hiker's Haven

If you're looking for a multi-day hiking experience, the Stubai High Trail is one of the most stunning in the region, stretching over 120 kilometers and taking you through some of Austria's most beautiful alpine landscapes. The trail offers various hut-to-hut accommodations where you can rest along the way.

- Cost: For a 7-day trek along the Stubai High Trail, accommodation at mountain huts can range from €30-€70 per night, depending on the hut and the season. Access to some trailheads may also require a small fee of €5-€10.

Patscherkofel – Explore a Legendary Mountain

As one of Innsbruck's most iconic mountains, Patscherkofel offers easy access via the Patscherkofel Cable Car. From there, you can choose from various scenic hiking trails, including the Olympia Trail, which passes by the 1964 Olympic Ski Jump.

- Cost: A return ticket for the Patscherkofel Cable Car is about €25. Hiking itself is free.

Mountain Biking

Innsbruck is a mecca for mountain bikers, with its vast network of trails catering to all skill levels. From challenging downhill rides to leisurely bike paths, the region offers something for every cycling enthusiast.

Bike Park Innsbruck – Thrills and Excitement

Located just outside the city, Bike Park Innsbruck offers a thrilling downhill experience. The park is designed for bikers who enjoy fast-paced trails and technical challenges, featuring various routes for both beginners and advanced riders.

- Cost: A day pass for the Bike Park Innsbruck costs around €38 per person. Rental equipment (bike, helmet) is available for approximately €40-€60 per day.

Innsbruck to Zirl – Scenic Cycling

For a more relaxed ride, you can cycle along the Innsbruck-Zirl bike path. This scenic, 13 km route follows the Inn River and offers picturesque views of the valley, with plenty of spots for a break or picnic along the way.

- Cost: The bike rental costs around €15-€30 per day, depending on the type of bike. The cycling path is free to use.

Paragliding and Hang Gliding

Innsbruck's breathtaking landscapes offer the perfect setting for high-flying adventures. Paragliding is an increasingly popular activity, giving you the chance to soar above the Alps and experience the mountains from an entirely different perspective.

Take Off from the Mountains

Tandem paragliding flights are available from Nordkette and Patscherkofel, where expert pilots will guide you as you glide above the city, valleys, and lakes.

- Cost: A tandem paragliding flight typically costs around €140-€180 for a 20-30 minute flight, depending on the location and operator.

Rafting and Canyon Swing

For those looking for adrenaline-packed water adventures, Innsbruck offers thrilling rafting and canyon swinging activities, perfect for summer fun.

Rafting on the Inn River

Rafting trips along the Inn River offer a mix of scenic views and exciting rapids. The river passes through beautiful valleys, and the rafting tours are suitable for beginners and families, as well as more advanced adventurers.

- Cost: A half-day rafting tour costs between €50-€75 per person, including gear and a guide.

Canyon Swinging – High-Flying Thrills

For a truly unique experience, canyon swinging in the Ötztal Valley offers a thrilling swing over a stunning canyon. It's an adrenaline-packed activity that provides a truly unforgettable experience.

- Cost: The Canyon Swing costs around €100-€120 per person for a single jump.

Lake Swimming and Water Activities

Innsbruck's surrounding lakes provide the perfect place to cool off during the summer months. If you want to swim, paddleboard, or just relax by the water, the alpine lakes around Innsbruck offer tranquility and beauty.

Lake Lans

Located just a short drive from Innsbruck, Lake Lans is ideal for a relaxing day by the water. You can swim in its clear waters, rent a paddleboard, or just enjoy a peaceful picnic along the shore.

- Cost: Access to Lake Lans is free. Paddleboard rental costs around €15 per hour.

Lake Natterer

Lake Natterer is another popular spot near Innsbruck, known for its crystal-clear waters and peaceful ambiance. It's perfect for a family day out, with activities like swimming and boating available.

- Cost: Access to Lake Natterer is free. Pedalo rental is about €15-€20 per hour.

Cultural Festivals and Events

Innsbruck comes alive in the summer with a wide range of cultural festivals and events. From classical music to contemporary art, there's something for every cultural enthusiast.

Innsbruck Festival of Early Music

The Innsbruck Festival of Early Music celebrates classical compositions from the Renaissance and Baroque periods, bringing world-class performances to the city. It's a highlight of the summer cultural calendar for music lovers.

- Cost: Tickets for performances range from €20 to €50, depending on the event.

Hofgarten Summer Concerts

Held in the beautiful Hofgarten Palace, the Hofgarten Summer Concerts feature a series of open-air classical music concerts, perfect for enjoying a relaxing evening in the heart of the city.

Best Areas to Stay

Altstadt (Old Town)

Stay in the Altstadt for a historic and central experience, with easy access to major attractions.

The Altstadt, or Old Town, is the historic heart of Innsbruck, where you'll find a charming blend of medieval and baroque architecture. This area is perfect for those who want to engage themselves in the city's history and culture. Key attractions like the Golden Roof, the Imperial Palace (Hofburg), and the Cathedral of St. James are all within walking distance. The narrow, cobblestone streets are lined with colorful buildings, quaint shops, and cozy cafes, making it a delightful area to explore.

Crowd Level: High. The Old Town is popular with tourists year-round, especially in the summer and during the Christmas market season.

Altstadt is ideal for first-time visitors and history enthusiasts who want to be in the midst of Innsbruck's most iconic sights and vibrant cultural scene.

Wilten

Choose Wilten for a mix of historical charm, green spaces, and a quieter residential atmosphere.

Wilten is a historic district located just south of the Old Town. It offers a peaceful, residential feel with beautiful churches, including the Wilten Basilica and the Wilten Abbey. The area is known for its green spaces, such as the Rapoldi Park and the picturesque Botanical Garden. Wilten is also home to the Bergisel Ski Jump, which offers stunning views over Innsbruck and the surrounding mountains.

Crowd Level: Moderate. Wilten is less crowded than the Old Town, offering a tranquil environment with fewer tourists.

Wilten is perfect for travelers seeking a quieter stay with easy access to green spaces and historical landmarks. It's also ideal for families and those who enjoy a more local, residential atmosphere.

Pradl

Stay in Pradl for a vibrant, multicultural neighborhood with excellent transport links and modern amenities.

Pradl is a lively district located east of the Old Town, known for its multicultural atmosphere and modern amenities. The area offers a variety of shops, cafes, and restaurants, reflecting a blend of different cultures. Pradl is also home to the Tivoli Stadium and the Olympiaworld sports complex, making it a great choice for sports enthusiasts. The district's excellent public transport connections make it easy to explore Innsbruck and its surroundings.

Crowd Level: Moderate. Pradl is a busy residential area with a steady flow of locals and visitors, but it's less touristy than the city center.

Pradl is great for travelers who appreciate a multicultural environment, modern amenities, and good transport links. It's ideal for those looking for a vibrant neighborhood with easy access to the rest of the city.

Hötting

Choose Hötting for a scenic and residential area with stunning views and easy access to nature.

Hötting is a picturesque district located northwest of the Old Town, known for its beautiful views of the Alps and its tranquil, residential feel. The area is perfect for nature lovers, offering numerous hiking and biking trails that start right from the neighborhood. Hötting is also home to the charming Höttinger Church and several traditional Austrian guesthouses.

Crowd Level: Low. Hötting is a quieter, more residential area with fewer tourists, providing a serene environment.

Hötting is perfect for travelers who want a peaceful retreat with beautiful scenery and outdoor activities. It's an excellent choice for families, nature lovers, and those seeking a more tranquil stay.

Cultural Sites

The Imperial Palace (Hofburg)

First up is the Imperial Palace, or Hofburg, a true gem in Innsbruck's cultural crown. This stunning palace was originally built in the 15th century and later remodeled in the baroque style by Empress Maria Theresa.

Key Exhibits and Collections:

State Apartments: Wander through the lavishly decorated state rooms, including the magnificent Giant's Hall with its grand frescoes and portraits of Habsburg royalty.

Maria Theresa's Rooms: Get a glimpse into the life of Empress Maria Theresa and her influence on the palace.

Palace Chapel: A beautifully preserved baroque chapel that offers a serene escape.

Practical Information:

- Opening Hours: Daily from 9:00 AM to 5:00 PM.
- Ticket Prices: Adults €9.50, reduced rates for children, students, and seniors.

Tips: Take a guided tour to learn fascinating stories about the Habsburgs and the palace's history. Don't forget your camera to capture the opulent interiors!

Ambras Castle (Schloss Ambras)

Next, let's head to Ambras Castle, located just a short distance from the city center. This Renaissance castle, built by Archduke Ferdinand II, is not only a historical treasure but also a museum housing an impressive array of collections.

Key Exhibits and Collections:

Spanish Hall: One of the most stunning Renaissance halls in the world, decorated with portraits of Tyrolean nobility.

Chamber of Art and Curiosities: An eclectic collection featuring armor, paintings, and exotic items from around the globe.

Bathing Chambers: Visit the beautifully preserved Renaissance bathing chambers.

Practical Information:

- Opening Hours: Daily from 10:00 AM to 5:00 PM (varies seasonally).
- Ticket Prices: Adults €12.00, reduced rates for children, students, and seniors.

Hofkirche (Court Church)

The Hofkirche, or Court Church, is a gothic masterpiece that houses one of the most important monuments of the Habsburg dynasty.

Key Exhibits and Collections:

Maximilian's Tomb: The centerpiece of the church is the elaborate tomb of Emperor Maximilian I, surrounded by 28 larger-than-life bronze statues of his ancestors and heroes.

Silver Chapel: Named for its silver altar, this chapel is dedicated to Archduke Ferdinand II and his wife, Philippine Welser.

Ebert Organ: One of the oldest playable organs in the world, dating back to the Renaissance.

Practical Information:

- Opening Hours: Monday to Saturday from 9:00 AM to 5:00 PM, Sunday from 12:30 PM to 6:00 PM.
- Ticket Prices: Adults €7.00, reduced rates for children, students, and seniors.

Tiroler Landesmuseum (Tyrolean State Museum)

Known locally as the Ferdinandeum, the Tiroler Landesmuseum is a must-visit for those interested in Tyrolean history and culture.

Key Exhibits and Collections:

Art Collections: From Gothic altarpieces to modern art, the museum's diverse collection showcases the artistic heritage of Tyrol.

Historical Artifacts: Explore archaeological finds, traditional costumes, and everyday objects that tell the story of Tyrolean life through the ages.

Music Room: A delightful exhibit featuring historical musical instruments and information on Tyrolean musical traditions.

Practical Information:

- Opening Hours: Tuesday to Sunday from 9:00 AM to 5:00 PM (closed on Mondays).
- Ticket Prices: Adults €11.00, reduced rates for children, students, and seniors.

Tiroler Volkskunstmuseum (Tyrolean Folk Art Museum)

Adjacent to the Hofkirche, the Tiroler Volkskunstmuseum offers a deep dive into the folk culture and traditions of Tyrol.

Key Exhibits and Collections:

Folk Art Collections: Traditional costumes, textiles, religious folk art, and household items provide a colorful look at Tyrolean life.

Reconstructed Parlors: Beautifully recreated traditional Tyrolean parlors showcase the region's rural life and architectural styles.

Seasonal Exhibits: The museum hosts seasonal exhibits related to Tyrolean customs and festivals.

Practical Information:

- Opening Hours: Daily from 9:00 AM to 5:00 PM.
- Ticket Prices: Adults €10.00, reduced rates for children, students, and seniors.

Bergisel Ski Jump

The Bergisel Ski Jump is an architectural marvel and a site of significant historical importance, having hosted the Winter Olympics in 1964 and 1976.

Key Exhibits and Collections:

Panoramic Views: Take the elevator to the top of the tower for breathtaking views of Innsbruck and the Alps.

Olympic History: Learn about the ski jump's role in the Winter Olympics and its significance in the world of winter sports.

Café and Restaurant: Enjoy a meal or drink at the café, which offers stunning panoramic views.

Practical Information:

- Opening Hours: Daily from 9:00 AM to 5:00 PM.

- Ticket Prices: Adults €10.00, reduced rates for children, students, and seniors.

Exploring Innsbruck

Altstadt (Old Town)

The heart of Innsbruck is its Altstadt, or Old Town, a beautifully preserved medieval area with narrow cobblestone streets, colorful buildings, and historical landmarks. Start your exploration at the Golden Roof (Goldenes Dachl), a striking building adorned with 2,657 gilded copper tiles. Built in the 15th century, it's now a museum dedicated to Emperor Maximilian I.

Wander through the Old Town and you'll come across the impressive Imperial Palace (Hofburg), once the residence of the Habsburgs. The palace boasts lavish state apartments and beautiful gardens. Nearby, the Hofkirche (Court Church) is home to the stunning black marble tomb of Emperor Maximilian I, flanked by 28 larger-than-life bronze statues.

Maria-Theresien-Straße

One of Innsbruck's main thoroughfares, Maria-Theresien-Straße, is a vibrant and bustling street lined with shops, cafes, and historical buildings. It's the perfect place to soak up the local atmosphere. The Annasäule (St. Anne's Column) stands proudly in the middle of the street, surrounded by the majestic Nordkette mountain range.

This area is also home to the iconic Triumphal Arch (Triumphpforte), built in the 18th century to commemorate a royal wedding. As you stroll along Maria-Theresien-Straße, you'll find a mix of high-end boutiques and charming local shops, perfect for a bit of retail therapy.

Nordkette and Seegrube

For breathtaking panoramic views of Innsbruck and the surrounding Alps, head to the Nordkette mountain range. The journey starts with a ride on the Hungerburgbahn funicular from the city center to Hungerburg. From there, a cable car takes you up to Seegrube and then further up to Hafelekar, at an altitude of over 2,200 meters.

At Seegrube, you can enjoy stunning views, dine at the mountaintop restaurant, and even partake in outdoor activities like hiking or skiing, depending on the season. The experience of being high above the city, with the Alps stretching out before you, is truly unforgettable.

Ambras Castle

A short distance from the city center, Ambras Castle (Schloss Ambras) is a Renaissance jewel set amidst beautiful gardens. This castle was the residence of Archduke Ferdinand II and is now a museum housing a remarkable collection of art, armor, and artifacts.

Explore the stunning Spanish Hall, one of the most beautiful Renaissance halls in the world, adorned with portraits of Tyrolean nobles. The castle's extensive gardens are perfect for a leisurely stroll, offering serene spots to relax and enjoy the scenery.

Hofgarten

If you're looking for a peaceful escape within the city, the Hofgarten is a beautifully landscaped park near the Old Town. Dating back to the 15th century, this park features mature trees, manicured lawns, and lovely flowerbeds. It's an ideal spot for a leisurely walk, a picnic, or simply to unwind with a book.

The park also hosts various events and concerts, especially in the summer months, adding a cultural touch to its tranquil environment.

Bergisel Ski Jump

For a blend of sports history and architectural brilliance, visit the Bergisel Ski Jump. Designed by famed architect Zaha Hadid, this modern ski jump is an impressive structure offering panoramic views of Innsbruck. The site also has a rich history, having hosted the Winter Olympics in 1964 and 1976.

Take the funicular and elevator to the top of the tower, where you can enjoy breathtaking views of the city and the surrounding mountains. The venue also features a café where you can relax and take in the scenery.

Wilten Abbey

For a touch of serenity and spiritual beauty, head to Wilten Abbey, a stunning baroque abbey church located in the Wilten district. The interior of the church is richly decorated with ornate stucco work, beautiful frescoes, and intricate altars. The abbey also has a peaceful courtyard garden that's perfect for contemplation.

GRAZ: AUSTRIA'S CULINARY CAPITAL

Historical and Modern Attractions

Altstadt (Old Town)

Graz's Old Town is a UNESCO World Heritage site and a living museum of architectural styles from the Gothic, Renaissance, Baroque, and modern periods. Walking through its narrow, winding streets feels like stepping back in time.

Key Highlights:

Hauptplatz: The main square, surrounded by beautiful historic buildings and the imposing Rathaus (Town Hall). This is a great starting point for exploring the Old Town.

Landhaus: This Renaissance masterpiece features a stunning arcaded courtyard and is home to the Styrian Provincial Parliament.

Glockenspiel: Don't miss the charming clock tower where, three times a day, mechanical figures come out to dance to traditional music.

Practical Information:

- Location: Central Graz, easily accessible on foot.
- Opening Hours: The Old Town itself is always open; specific sites like the Landhaus have variable hours (typically 10:00 AM - 6:00 PM).
- Ticket Prices: Free to explore the Old Town. Individual sites may charge entry (e.g., Landhaus: Adults €2.00).

Schlossberg and Uhrturm

The Schlossberg, a hill in the center of Graz, is home to the city's iconic Uhrturm (Clock Tower). This area offers stunning views of Graz and is rich with history.

Key Highlights:

Uhrturm: The Clock Tower, with its unique reversed clock hands (the hour hand is larger than the minute hand), is a symbol of Graz.

Schlossberg Stairs: Climb the 260 steps for a scenic workout, or take the funicular or lift if you prefer a more leisurely ascent.

Kriegssteig: A historic path built during WWI that leads to the top of Schlossberg.

Practical Information:

- Location: Accessible from the city center; entrances at Schlossbergplatz or via the funicular/lift.
- Opening Hours: Open 24/7, but the funicular and lift operate from 9:00 AM to 10:00 PM.
- Ticket Prices: Access to Schlossberg is free; funicular and lift cost around €2.40 for a one-way trip.

Graz Cathedral and Mausoleum

The Graz Cathedral (Dom) and Mausoleum of Emperor Ferdinand II are two of the most important religious sites in the city, showcasing beautiful Gothic and Baroque architecture.

Key Highlights:

Graz Cathedral: This Gothic church is known for its beautiful frescoes and baroque altars.

Mausoleum of Emperor Ferdinand II: Located next to the cathedral, this baroque masterpiece features an impressive façade and grand dome.

Practical Information:

- Location: Located in the Old Town, near the Burg.

- Opening Hours: Graz Cathedral: Daily from 7:00 AM to 7:00 PM; Mausoleum: Daily from 10:00 AM to 4:00 PM.
- Ticket Prices: Graz Cathedral: Free entry; Mausoleum: Adults €5.50, reduced rates for children, students, and seniors.

Kunsthaus Graz (Art Museum)

Kunsthaus Graz, affectionately known as the "Friendly Alien" due to its distinctive blob-like shape, is a contemporary art museum that stands in stark contrast to Graz's historic architecture.

Key Highlights:

Exhibitions: The museum hosts rotating exhibitions of contemporary art, featuring works by local and international artists.

Architecture: Designed by Peter Cook and Colin Fournier, the building itself is a work of art, with its unique biomorphic design and striking blue façade.

Needle: An observation deck offering panoramic views of the city.

Practical Information:

- Location: Lendkai 1, near the Mur River.
- Opening Hours: Tuesday to Sunday from 10:00 AM to 6:00 PM.
- Ticket Prices: Adults €9.00, reduced rates for children, students, and seniors.

Murinsel (Mur Island)

Murinsel, a futuristic floating platform in the middle of the Mur River, is one of Graz's most unique modern attractions.

Key Highlights:

Architecture: Designed by artist Vito Acconci, Murinsel features a café, an amphitheater, and a playground.

Café: Enjoy a coffee or a snack while taking in views of the river.

Amphitheater: Check out the schedule for performances and events held in this unique venue.

Practical Information:

- Location: Located in the Mur River, accessible from both banks.
- Opening Hours: Open daily, 24 hours.
- Ticket Prices: Free to enter; café and event prices vary.

Joanneumsviertel

Joanneumsviertel is a cultural complex that houses several important museums, including the Neue Galerie (New Gallery), the Natural History Museum, and the CoSA – Center of Science Activities.

Key Highlights:

Neue Galerie: Features modern and contemporary art collections.

Natural History Museum: Offers fascinating exhibits on geology, paleontology, and zoology.

CoSA: An interactive science center perfect for families and curious minds.

Practical Information:

- Location: Raubergasse 10.
- Opening Hours: Tuesday to Sunday from 10:00 AM to 5:00 PM.
- Ticket Prices: Combined ticket for all museums: Adults €11.00, reduced rates for children, students, and seniors.

Best Places to Stay

Inner City (Innere Stadt)

Stay in the Inner City for a historic and cultural experience at the heart of Graz.

The Inner City, or Innere Stadt, is the historic core of Graz and a UNESCO World Heritage site. It's where you'll find most of the city's major attractions, including the Graz Cathedral, the Mausoleum of Emperor Ferdinand II, and the iconic Clock Tower on Schlossberg Hill. The area is characterized by its cobblestone streets, beautiful squares, and impressive architecture. Staying here means you're within walking distance of museums, galleries, theaters, as well as a variety of cafes, restaurants, and shops.

Crowd Level: High. The Inner City attracts both tourists and locals, especially around popular sights and shopping streets. However, its central location and historical significance make it worth the crowds.

You'll be engaged in Graz's history and culture, with easy access to the city's top attractions, dining, and shopping. It's ideal for first-time visitors and those who want to be at the center of Graz's vibrant city life.

Lend

Choose Lend for a trendy and artistic vibe close to the city center.

Lend is an up-and-coming district known for its creative spirit and vibrant atmosphere. Just across the Mur River from the Inner City, Lend offers a mix of modern art galleries, hip cafes, and trendy boutiques. The district's centerpiece is the Lendplatz market, a bustling hub of activity with fresh produce, street food, and local crafts.

Crowd Level: Moderate. Lend is popular among locals and younger visitors, particularly around the market and art venues. It's lively but not as crowded as the Inner City.

Lend is perfect for those who appreciate modern culture and creativity. It's an excellent choice for art lovers, fashion enthusiasts, and anyone looking to experience Graz's contemporary side.

Geidorf

Stay in Geidorf for a peaceful residential area with easy access to nature and the city center.

Geidorf is a leafy, residential district located just north of the Inner City. It's known for its beautiful parks, historic villas, and proximity to the University of Graz. The district offers a quiet, relaxed environment, making it an ideal choice for families and those seeking a peaceful stay.

Crowd Level: Low. Geidorf is predominantly a residential area, offering a tranquil environment away from the tourist crowds.

Geidorf is perfect for travelers who enjoy green spaces and a quieter, more residential environment. Its proximity to the city center and natural attractions makes it a great choice for families and those looking to relax.

Jakomini

Opt for Jakomini for a bustling district with great transport links and modern amenities.

Jakomini is a dynamic district situated southeast of the Inner City. It's known for its excellent public transportation connections and a wide range of shops, cafes, and entertainment options. Jakomini is also home to Graz's main train station, making it a convenient base for exploring the city and beyond.

Crowd Level: Moderate to High. Jakomini's transportation hub and entertainment options attract a steady flow of people, making it one of the busier districts in Graz.

Jakomini is great for travelers who prioritize convenience and accessibility. It's perfect for those who want to explore both the local area and further afield, with excellent transport links and a lively atmosphere.

Exploring Graz

Altstadt (Old Town)

The Altstadt, or Old Town, is the beating heart of Graz and a UNESCO World Heritage site. This area is renowned for its well-preserved medieval and Renaissance architecture. Start your exploration at the Hauptplatz, the main square, where you'll find the stunning Rathaus (Town Hall). The square is surrounded by beautiful buildings and bustling cafes, making it a perfect spot to soak up the atmosphere.

Just a short walk from the Hauptplatz is the Landhaus, a Renaissance masterpiece with a beautiful arcaded courtyard. The adjacent Styrian Armoury (Landeszeughaus) houses the world's largest historical armory collection, offering a fascinating glimpse into the past.

Schlossberg and Uhrturm

A visit to Graz isn't complete without ascending the Schlossberg, the hill that rises above the city. The Schlossberg is home to the iconic Uhrturm (Clock Tower), which offers panoramic views of the city. You can reach the top via a funicular railway, an elevator, or by climbing the 260-step Schlossbergstiege (Schlossberg Stairs).

At the summit, you'll find lush gardens, historic fortifications, and several cafes where you can relax and enjoy the view. The Uhrturm itself is a symbol of Graz, and its unique clock face, with the hour hand larger than the minute hand, is a curiosity.

Murinsel and Kunsthaus Graz

For a taste of Graz's modern side, head to the Murinsel and Kunsthaus Graz. The Murinsel, or Mur Island, is a futuristic floating platform in the middle of the Mur River. Designed by artist Vito Acconci, this artificial island features a cafe, an amphitheater, and a playground, making it a fun and unique place to visit.

Nearby, the Kunsthaus Graz, affectionately known as the "Friendly Alien," is a striking contemporary art museum. Its blob-like, blue exterior stands in stark contrast to the traditional buildings around it. Inside, you'll find cutting-edge exhibitions and installations from contemporary artists around the world.

Herrengasse and the Painted House

Herrengasse is one of Graz's main shopping streets, lined with elegant shops, cafes, and historical buildings. As you stroll down Herrengasse, be sure to stop by the Gemaltes Haus (Painted House) at number 3. This unique building is covered in intricate frescoes depicting mythological scenes, making it a true work of art.

The street is also home to the beautiful Gothic Franciscan Church and the Landhaushof, the courtyard of the Landhaus, which is particularly enchanting with its Renaissance arcades and fountains.

Graz Cathedral and Mausoleum

For a dose of spirituality and history, visit the Graz Cathedral (Dom), a stunning Gothic church dating back to the 15th century. The interior is adorned with beautiful frescoes and baroque altars. Next to the cathedral is the Mausoleum of Emperor Ferdinand II, a striking example of early baroque architecture with its elaborate façade and grand dome.

Stadtpark and Schloss Eggenberg

Graz offers plenty of green spaces to relax and enjoy nature. The Stadtpark, located near the Old Town, is a favorite among locals and visitors alike. This large park features beautiful lawns, statues, and fountains, making it perfect for a leisurely stroll or a picnic.

A bit further afield, Schloss Eggenberg is a baroque palace surrounded by expansive gardens. The palace is a UNESCO World Heritage site and offers guided tours of its lavish state rooms and impressive art collections. The surrounding park is home to peacocks and various sculptures, providing a serene escape from the city.

Farmers' Markets and Culinary Delights

Graz is known for its vibrant culinary scene, heavily influenced by the rich agricultural heritage of Styria. Visit one of the many farmers' markets, such as the Kaiser-Josef-Markt, to sample fresh local produce, cheeses, meats, and more. These markets are perfect for grabbing some snacks or ingredients for a picnic.

The city is also home to numerous traditional restaurants and wine taverns where you can enjoy Styrian specialties like pumpkin seed oil, hearty soups, and schnitzel. Don't miss trying a glass of local wine or a pint of Styrian beer.

OTHER NOTABLE DESTINATIONS

Hallstatt

Hallstatt is often described as one of the oldest and most beautiful villages in Austria. Its history dates back to prehistoric times, with archaeological evidence showing it was a significant center for salt production. In fact, Hallstatt's salt mines are some of the oldest in the world, with a history spanning over 7,000 years. This long history of salt mining has shaped the village's culture and economy, earning it a spot on the UNESCO World Heritage list.

As you wander through Hallstatt, you'll notice the charming wooden houses, narrow alleyways, and quaint squares that have remained largely unchanged for centuries. The village's name itself is derived from the Celtic word for salt, reflecting its long-standing importance in the region.

Key Highlights

Hallstatt Salt Mine (Salzwelten Hallstatt): One of the most fascinating attractions in Hallstatt is its ancient salt mine. Take a guided tour to explore the underground tunnels, learn about the history of salt mining, and even slide down a miner's slide. The tour also includes a ride on a funicular railway, which offers stunning views of the village and the lake.

Hallstatt Skywalk: For breathtaking panoramic views of Hallstatt and the surrounding Alps, head to the Hallstatt Skywalk. This viewing platform extends out over a cliff, offering a bird's-eye view of the village and the serene lake below. It's the perfect spot for capturing those postcard-worthy photos.

Bone House (Beinhaus) in St. Michael's Chapel: This might sound a bit eerie, but the Bone House is a unique and fascinating site. Due to limited burial space, the remains of villagers were exhumed, and their skulls were decorated and placed in the Bone House. It's a somber yet intriguing glimpse into Hallstatt's past.

Hallstatt Museum: To dive deeper into the village's history, visit the Hallstatt Museum. It showcases artifacts from the prehistoric era, the Hallstatt culture, and the history of salt mining. The exhibits are well-curated and provide a comprehensive understanding of the area's rich heritage.

Hallstätter See: The lake itself is a major attraction. Rent a boat or take a leisurely walk along the shoreline to enjoy the stunning scenery. The crystal-clear waters reflect the surrounding mountains, creating a picture-perfect setting.

Practical Information

Getting to Hallstatt is part of the adventure. You can take a train from Salzburg or Vienna to Attnang-Puchheim, then transfer to a local train to Hallstatt station. From there, a short ferry ride will take you across the lake to the village. The journey is scenic and adds to the charm of your visit.

Most attractions in Hallstatt are open year-round, but hours can vary, especially in the off-season. The salt mine tours typically run from 9:00 AM to 4:30 PM, while the museum is open from 10:00 AM to 5:00 PM. It's a good idea to check the specific opening hours for each site before your visit.

Zell am See

Zell am See's history dates back to Roman times, but it was officially founded in the 8th century as "Cella in Bisonzio." The town has grown from a modest settlement into a popular tourist destination, known for its breathtaking landscapes and year-round outdoor activities. The region's alpine culture is reflected in its traditional architecture, local festivals, and warm hospitality.

The town is centered around its beautiful lake, Zeller See, which is surrounded by the majestic peaks of the Hohe Tauern mountain range. This idyllic setting has made Zell am See a beloved destination for both summer and winter tourism, offering everything from skiing and snowboarding to hiking and water sports.

Key Highlights

Lake Zell (Zeller See): The sparkling Zeller See is the heart of Zell am See. The lake's crystal-clear waters are perfect for swimming, boating, and paddleboarding in the summer. In winter, the frozen lake becomes a playground for ice skating and curling. Take a leisurely boat cruise to enjoy the stunning scenery from a different perspective.

Schmittenhöhe Mountain: For panoramic views and outdoor adventures, head to Schmittenhöhe. This mountain is a paradise for skiers and snowboarders in the winter, with over 70 kilometers of slopes. In the summer, it transforms into a hiking and paragliding hotspot. The Schmittenhöhebahn cable car makes it easy to reach the summit, where you'll be rewarded with breathtaking views of the surrounding Alps and the lake below.

Kitzsteinhorn Glacier: Just a short drive from Zell am See, the Kitzsteinhorn Glacier offers year-round skiing and snowboarding. At an elevation of over 3,000 meters, you can enjoy snow sports even in the middle of summer. The Gipfelwelt 3000 viewing platform provides awe-inspiring vistas of the Hohe Tauern National Park.

Historic Town Center: Stroll through the charming streets of Zell am See's historic center, where you'll find traditional alpine buildings, cozy cafes, and local shops. Don't miss the 11th-century St. Hippolyte's Church, which features a unique Romanesque tower and beautiful frescoes.

Sigmund-Thun-Klamm: For a dose of natural beauty and adventure, visit Sigmund-Thun-Klamm, a stunning gorge carved by the Kapruner Ache river. Wooden walkways and bridges lead you through the gorge, offering close-up views of the rushing water and dramatic rock formations.

Practical Information

Zell am See is easily accessible by train from major Austrian cities like Salzburg and Vienna. The journey from Salzburg takes about 1.5 hours by train. If you're driving, Zell am See is well-connected by road, and there are plenty of parking facilities in town.

Zell am See is a year-round destination, with activities and attractions available in all seasons. Most shops and restaurants in the town center are open from around 9:00 AM to 6:00 PM. The Schmittenhöhe and Kitzsteinhorn lifts operate daily, with varying hours depending on the season.

Klagenfurt

Klagenfurt, officially known as Klagenfurt am Wörthersee, has a rich history that dates back to the 12th century. The city was founded by the Duke of Carinthia and has grown from a modest settlement into a bustling cultural and economic hub. Klagenfurt has endured fires, floods, and earthquakes over the centuries, but it has always been rebuilt and restored, often with even greater splendor.

Today, Klagenfurt is a city that beautifully blends its historical heritage with modern vibrancy. Its old town is a treasure trove of Renaissance and Baroque architecture, while the surrounding area offers stunning natural beauty, making it a perfect destination for both history buffs and nature lovers.

Key Highlights

Lake Wörthersee: One of the most beautiful and warmest alpine lakes in Austria, Lake Wörthersee is a major highlight of Klagenfurt. The turquoise waters are perfect for swimming, boating, and paddleboarding in the summer. There are numerous beaches and lidos around the lake where you can relax and soak up the sun. A boat tour on the lake is a must to fully appreciate its beauty.

Minimundus: For a unique and fun experience, visit Minimundus, the "miniature world" park located just outside Klagenfurt. This park features over 150 miniature models of famous buildings and landmarks from around the world, including the Eiffel Tower, the Statue of Liberty, and the Taj Mahal. It's a great place for families and offers a fascinating way to see the world in a day.

Lindwurm Fountain: Located in the heart of Klagenfurt's old town, the Lindwurm Fountain is a symbol of the city. The statue depicts a legendary dragon, the Lindwurm, which according to local legend, was defeated by the town's founders. The fountain is a popular meeting point and a great spot for photos.

Landhaus and Wappensaal: The Landhaus is one of Klagenfurt's most important historical buildings. This Renaissance palace houses the Carinthian State Parliament. Inside, you'll find the Wappensaal (Hall of Coats of Arms), which is adorned with stunning frescoes depicting the coats of arms of Carinthian noble families. The intricate artwork and historical significance make it a must-visit.

Kreuzbergl Nature Park: For a dose of nature within the city, head to Kreuzbergl Nature Park. This green oasis offers scenic walking trails, beautiful ponds, and panoramic views of Klagenfurt and the surrounding mountains. It's a perfect spot for a leisurely hike or a peaceful picnic.

Klagenfurt Cathedral: Also known as the Cathedral of Saints Peter and Paul, this Baroque cathedral is a stunning example of religious architecture. The interior is richly decorated with frescoes, altars, and ornate chapels. It's a serene and beautiful place to visit and reflect.

Gustav Mahler Composer's Cottage: Located near Lake Wörthersee, this charming cottage was the summer residence of the famous composer Gustav Mahler. Today, it's a museum dedicated to his life and work. Music lovers will enjoy the exhibits and the chance to see where Mahler composed some of his greatest works.

Practical Information

Klagenfurt is well-connected by train and road. You can easily reach it by train from major Austrian cities like Vienna, Graz, and Salzburg. Klagenfurt also has its own airport, with flights connecting to several European destinations.

Most attractions in Klagenfurt have variable opening hours, especially in the off-season. For example:

- Minimundus: Typically open daily from 9:00 AM to 6:00 PM.
- Landhaus and Wappensaal: Open weekdays from 10:00 AM to 2:00 PM.
- Gustav Mahler Composer's Cottage: Open from May to October, daily from 10:00 AM to 5:00 PM.

Ticket Prices:

- Minimundus: Adults €19.00, reduced rates for children, students, and seniors.
- Landhaus and Wappensaal: Entrance is often free, but guided tours may have a small fee.
- Gustav Mahler Composer's Cottage: Adults €6.00, reduced rates for children, students, and seniors.

Linz

Linz has a rich history that dates back to Roman times when it was known as "Lentia." Over the centuries, it has evolved from a small settlement into a major industrial and cultural hub. Linz played a significant role during the Habsburg era and later became an important center for the steel and chemical industries. Today, Linz is renowned for its dynamic blend of history, technology, and culture, making it a fascinating place to explore.

The city's transformation is epitomized by its designation as a UNESCO City of Media Arts, reflecting its commitment to innovation and creativity. Linz offers a unique mix of historical sites, cutting-edge museums, and vibrant cultural events that attract visitors from all over the world.

Key Highlights

Ars Electronica Center: Known as the "Museum of the Future," the Ars Electronica Center is a must-visit for anyone interested in technology and innovation. This interactive museum explores the intersection of art, technology, and society. You can experience futuristic exhibits, virtual reality installations, and hands-on workshops that showcase the latest advancements in science and digital art.

Lentos Art Museum: Located along the Danube River, the Lentos Art Museum is one of Austria's most important modern art museums. It houses an impressive collection of 20th and 21st-century art, including works by Gustav Klimt, Egon Schiele, and Andy Warhol. The museum's striking modern architecture and riverside location make it a highlight of any visit to Linz.

Old Cathedral (Alter Dom): The Old Cathedral, also known as the Ignatiuskirche, is a beautiful baroque church located in the heart of Linz's historic old town. Its ornate interior, with stunning frescoes and a magnificent organ, is a testament to baroque craftsmanship. The cathedral also hosts regular concerts, adding a musical dimension to your visit.

New Cathedral (Mariendom): The New Cathedral, or Mariendom, is the largest church in Austria and a masterpiece of neo-Gothic architecture. Its towering spires and intricate stained glass windows create an awe-inspiring atmosphere. Climb the tower for panoramic views of the city and the Danube River.

Hauptplatz and Trinity Column: The Hauptplatz, or Main Square, is the vibrant heart of Linz. This expansive square is surrounded by historic buildings, cafes, and shops. At its center stands the Trinity Column, a baroque monument that commemorates the city's deliverance from plague, fire, and war. The Hauptplatz is a great place to start your exploration of Linz's old town.

Schlossmuseum Linz: Perched on a hill overlooking the city, the Schlossmuseum Linz offers a fascinating journey through Upper Austria's history. The museum's extensive collections include artifacts from prehistoric times to the present day. Don't miss the beautiful gardens and panoramic views from the castle grounds.

Pöstlingberg: For a scenic escape, take a trip to Pöstlingberg, a hill that offers stunning views of Linz and the surrounding countryside. The Pöstlingbergbahn, one of the steepest adhesion railways in Europe, will take you to the top. At the summit, you'll find the Pöstlingberg Basilica, a charming pilgrimage church, and the Grottenbahn, a whimsical cave railway that's perfect for families.

Practical Information

Linz is well-connected by train, with frequent services from major Austrian cities like Vienna, Salzburg, and Graz. The city also has its own airport, Blue Danube Airport Linz, which offers flights to several

European destinations. If you're driving, Linz is easily accessible via the A1 and A7 motorways.

Opening Hours:

- Ars Electronica Center: Open daily from 10:00 AM to 6:00 PM.
- Lentos Art Museum: Open Tuesday to Sunday from 10:00 AM to 6:00 PM, and Thursdays until 9:00 PM.
- Old Cathedral: Open daily from 7:00 AM to 7:00 PM.
- New Cathedral: Open daily from 8:00 AM to 6:00 PM.
- Schlossmuseum Linz: Open Tuesday to Sunday from 10:00 AM to 6:00 PM.

Ticket Prices:

- Ars Electronica Center: Adults €9.50, reduced rates for children, students, and seniors.
- Lentos Art Museum: Adults €8.00, reduced rates for children, students, and seniors.
- Schlossmuseum Linz: Adults €8.00, reduced rates for children, students, and seniors.

OUTDOOR ADVENTURES

Hiking and Mountaineering

The Austrian Alps

The Austrian Alps are renowned for their stunning scenery, diverse landscapes, and well-maintained trail networks. If you're a seasoned mountaineer or a casual hiker, there's something for everyone in these majestic mountains.

Key Hiking and Mountaineering Destinations

Tirol

The Tirol region is a top destination for hiking and mountaineering, boasting some of the most spectacular mountain scenery in Austria.

Stubai Valley:

- Location: Stubai Valley, near Innsbruck.
- Difficulty Level: Easy to Difficult.
- Highlights: The Stubai Glacier, the Stubai High Trail, and numerous waterfalls.

Tips: Stay in mountain huts (Almhütten) along the trail for an authentic alpine experience. Check the weather forecast before you start, as conditions can change rapidly in the mountains.

Salzburg and Berchtesgaden

The Salzburg region and nearby Berchtesgaden National Park offer some of Austria's most picturesque hiking trails.

Grossglockner High Alpine Road:

- Location: Hohe Tauern National Park.

- Difficulty Level: Moderate to Difficult.
- Highlights: Grossglockner, Austria's highest peak, and the scenic high alpine road.

Tips: Bring sturdy hiking boots and plenty of water. The trails can be steep and rocky, so be prepared for a workout.

Vorarlberg

Vorarlberg, located in the westernmost part of Austria, is known for its diverse landscapes and excellent hiking opportunities.

Lechweg Trail:

- Location: Arlberg region, starting in Lech am Arlberg.
- Difficulty Level: Easy to Moderate.
- Highlights: Alpine meadows, deep gorges, and picturesque villages.

Carinthia

Carinthia, located in southern Austria, offers a blend of alpine and Mediterranean climates, making it a unique destination for hiking and mountaineering.

Carnic High Trail:

- Location: Along the border between Austria and Italy.
- Difficulty Level: Moderate to Difficult.
- Highlights: Stunning views of the Carnic Alps, alpine huts, and diverse flora and fauna.

The Dachstein Mountains

The Dachstein Mountains, part of the Northern Limestone Alps, are a UNESCO World Heritage site and offer some of Austria's most dramatic landscapes.

Dachstein Glacier:

- Location: Near Hallstatt and Ramsau am Dachstein.
- Difficulty Level: Moderate to Difficult.
- Highlights: Dachstein Ice Palace, Sky Walk, Suspension Bridge, and Dachstein Crossing.

Tips: Wear sun protection, as the glacier reflects sunlight intensely. Bring crampons if you plan to hike on the glacier.

Skiing and Snowboarding

Austria is a skier's paradise. The country boasts some of the most famous ski resorts in the world, with a perfect mix of challenging runs, family-friendly slopes, and off-piste adventures. The stunning Alpine scenery, well-maintained pistes, and excellent facilities make it a top destination for winter sports enthusiasts.

Top Ski Resorts in Austria

St. Anton am Arlberg

Known as the cradle of alpine skiing, St. Anton is legendary. It's famous for its extensive terrain, deep powder, and vibrant après-ski scene.

Highlights:

- Ski Area: 305 kilometers of marked runs, plus 200 kilometers of off-piste trails.
- Difficulty Level: Suitable for intermediate to expert skiers and snowboarders.
- Après-Ski: The MooserWirt and Krazy Kanguruh are iconic spots for après-ski fun.

Practical Information:

- Location: Tyrol region, western Austria.

- Best Time to Visit: December to April.

Kitzbühel

Kitzbühel combines tradition with glamour. It's home to the famous Hahnenkamm race, one of the most challenging downhill races in the world.

Highlights:

- Ski Area: 185 kilometers of pistes.
- Difficulty Level: Suitable for all levels, with a good mix of easy, intermediate, and challenging runs.
- Après-Ski: Enjoy the nightlife at places like The Londoner and Highways.

Practical Information:

- Location: Tyrol region, eastern Austria.
- Best Time to Visit: December to March.

Tips: Try to catch the Hahnenkamm race in January for an unforgettable experience. Don't forget to explore the charming medieval town center.

Ischgl

Ischgl is renowned for its extensive ski area and its legendary après-ski and nightlife. The resort is linked with Samnaun in Switzerland, offering a vast skiing playground.

Highlights:

- Ski Area: 239 kilometers of pistes.
- Difficulty Level: Mostly intermediate, but plenty of options for beginners and experts too.
- Après-Ski: Check out the Trofana Alm and the Pacha nightclub.

Practical Information:

- Location: Tyrol region, western Austria.
- Best Time to Visit: November to May.

Sölden

Sölden is famous for its long ski season, glacier skiing, and as a venue for the Alpine Ski World Cup.

Highlights:

- Ski Area: 144 kilometers of pistes.
- Difficulty Level: All levels, with excellent glacier skiing.
- Après-Ski: Fire & Ice and the Schirmbar are popular après-ski spots.

Practical Information:

- Location: Tyrol region, Ötztal Valley.
- Best Time to Visit: October to May.

Tips: Visit the James Bond experience at the top of the Gaislachkogl, where scenes from "Spectre" were filmed.

Watersports

Austria's pristine lakes, crystal-clear rivers, and picturesque landscapes make it an ideal destination for watersports enthusiasts. If you're into kayaking, paddleboarding, windsurfing, or simply enjoying a peaceful boat ride, Austria's diverse waterways offer endless opportunities for fun and adventure.

Lake Wolfgang (Wolfgangsee)

Lake Wolfgang is one of Austria's most popular lakes, known for its stunning turquoise waters and charming lakeside villages.

Watersports:

- Paddleboarding: Glide across the calm waters and enjoy the scenic beauty.
- Windsurfing: The lake's favorable wind conditions make it a hotspot for windsurfing.
- Kayaking: Explore the lake's hidden coves and serene shoreline.

Practical Information:

- Location: Salzkammergut region, near Salzburg.
- Best Time to Visit: May to September.

Lake Neusiedl (Neusiedler See)

Lake Neusiedl is a UNESCO World Heritage site and Europe's largest steppe lake, offering excellent conditions for a variety of watersports.

Watersports:

- Windsurfing and Kitesurfing: The consistent winds make it ideal for both beginners and advanced surfers.
- Sailing: Rent a sailboat and enjoy the vast expanse of the lake.
- Canoeing: Paddle through the reed-lined shores and spot local wildlife.

Practical Information:

- Location: Burgenland, near the Hungarian border.
- Best Time to Visit: April to October.

Lake Wolfgangsee (Wörthersee)

Lake Wörthersee is another gem in Carinthia, famous for its warm, clear waters and vibrant summer scene.

Watersports:

- Wakeboarding and Water Skiing: The calm waters are perfect for thrilling wakeboarding and water skiing sessions.

- Stand-Up Paddleboarding (SUP): Enjoy a leisurely paddle while taking in the stunning alpine backdrop.
- Swimming: The lake's warm waters make it a favorite for swimmers.

Practical Information:

- Location: Carinthia, near Klagenfurt.
- Best Time to Visit: June to September.

Tips: Visit the vibrant town of Velden for lively beach clubs and watersport rentals. The annual Ironman Austria triathlon takes place here, adding to the excitement.

River Salza

For those seeking a more adrenaline-pumping experience, the River Salza offers some of the best white-water rafting and kayaking in Austria.

Watersports:

- White-Water Rafting: Navigate through thrilling rapids and enjoy the stunning gorge scenery.
- Kayaking: Experience the river's clear waters and exciting rapids in a kayak.

Practical Information:

- Location: Styria region.
- Best Time to Visit: May to September.

Lake Hallstatt (Hallstätter See)

Lake Hallstatt is a serene and picturesque lake, perfect for a more relaxed watersports experience.

Watersports:

- Canoeing and Kayaking: Paddle through the tranquil waters surrounded by mountains and charming villages.
- Stand-Up Paddleboarding (SUP): Explore the lake at your own pace on a paddleboard.
- Scuba Diving: Discover the underwater world and historical artifacts submerged in the lake.

Practical Information:

- Location: Salzkammergut region.
- Best Time to Visit: May to September.

Cycling Trails

Austria's diverse terrain, beautiful scenery, and excellent cycling infrastructure make it a top destination for cyclists. The country's extensive network of cycling paths is well-marked and often passes through breathtaking landscapes, historical sites, and quaint villages. If you're looking for a relaxing day trip or an epic multi-day adventure, Austria has something to offer every cyclist.

Danube Cycle Path (Donauradweg)

The Danube Cycle Path is one of Europe's most popular long-distance cycling routes, following the majestic Danube River from Germany to the Black Sea. The Austrian section, from Passau to Vienna, is particularly stunning.

Highlights:

- Scenic Views: Enjoy picturesque river landscapes, lush vineyards, and charming towns.
- Historical Sites: Visit Melk Abbey, the Wachau Valley (a UNESCO World Heritage site), and the city of Linz.

- Family-Friendly: The path is mostly flat and well-paved, making it suitable for cyclists of all ages and skill levels.

Practical Information:

- Location: Passau (Germany) to Vienna (Austria).
- Distance: Approximately 300 kilometers.
- Best Time to Visit: May to October.

Tauern Cycle Path (Tauernradweg)

The Tauern Cycle Path takes you through the heart of the Austrian Alps, from Krimml to Passau, following the Salzach and Inn rivers.

Highlights:

- Natural Beauty: Ride through the Hohe Tauern National Park, past the stunning Krimml Waterfalls, and along scenic river valleys.
- Cultural Stops: Explore the historic cities of Salzburg and Burghausen.
- Diverse Terrain: Enjoy a mix of flat sections and gentle inclines, with a few challenging stretches.

Practical Information:

- Location: Krimml to Passau.
- Distance: Approximately 310 kilometers.
- Best Time to Visit: May to October.

Salzkammergut Cycle Path

The Salzkammergut Cycle Path takes you through the picturesque Salzkammergut region, known for its crystal-clear lakes, rolling hills, and charming villages.

Highlights:

- Lake District: Cycle around beautiful lakes such as Wolfgangsee, Hallstätter See, and Traunsee.
- Historic Towns: Visit the UNESCO World Heritage town of Hallstatt and the spa town of Bad Ischl.
- Varied Scenery: Enjoy a mix of lakeside paths, forest trails, and mountain views.

Practical Information:

- Location: Loop through the Salzkammergut region.
- Distance: Approximately 345 kilometers (various route options).
- Best Time to Visit: May to October.

Alpe-Adria Cycle Path

The Alpe-Adria Cycle Path is a stunning cross-border route that takes you from the Austrian Alps to the Adriatic Sea in Italy.

Highlights:

- Alpine Landscapes: Start your journey in Salzburg and ride through the beautiful Hohe Tauern mountains.
- Cultural Experiences: Pass through historic towns such as Villach and the Italian cities of Udine and Grado.
- Scenic Transition: Experience the transition from alpine scenery to Mediterranean landscapes.

Practical Information:

- Location: Salzburg (Austria) to Grado (Italy).
- Distance: Approximately 410 kilometers.
- Best Time to Visit: May to October.

Inn Cycle Path (Innradweg)

The Inn Cycle Path follows the Inn River from its source in Switzerland, through Austria, to Passau in Germany.

Highlights:

- Riverside Views: Enjoy scenic river landscapes and lush valleys.
- Historic Cities: Visit Innsbruck, with its stunning alpine backdrop, and the charming towns of Kufstein and Passau.
- Diverse Terrain: The route offers a mix of flat and hilly sections, suitable for intermediate cyclists.

Practical Information:

- Location: Maloja (Switzerland) to Passau (Germany), through Austria.
- Distance: Approximately 520 kilometers.
- Best Time to Visit: May to October.

CULTURAL AND HISTORICAL TOURS

Castles and Palaces

Schönbrunn Palace (Schloss Schönbrunn)

Schönbrunn Palace in Vienna is one of Austria's most iconic landmarks. This former summer residence of the Habsburg dynasty is a UNESCO World Heritage site and a masterpiece of Baroque architecture.

Highlights:

Palace Tour: Explore the lavish state rooms and private apartments, including the magnificent Great Gallery and the Hall of Mirrors.

Gardens: Stroll through the beautifully landscaped gardens, complete with fountains, statues, and the impressive Neptune Fountain.

Gloriette: Climb to the Gloriette for panoramic views of the palace and Vienna.

Practical Information:

- Location: Schönbrunner Schloßstraße 47, 1130 Vienna, Austria.
- Opening Hours: Daily from 8:00 AM to 5:30 PM (hours may vary seasonally).
- Ticket Prices: Adults €22.00, reduced rates for children, students, and seniors.
- Phone: +43 1 811 13-239

Hohensalzburg Fortress (Festung Hohensalzburg)

Perched on a hill overlooking the city of Salzburg, Hohensalzburg Fortress is one of Europe's largest and best-preserved medieval castles.

Highlights:

Medieval Rooms: Discover the impressive medieval chambers, including the Golden Hall and the Golden Chamber.

Fortress Museum: Learn about the history of the fortress and its role in the defense of Salzburg.

Panoramic Views: Enjoy breathtaking views of Salzburg and the surrounding Alps from the fortress walls.

Practical Information:

- Location: Mönchsberg 34, 5020 Salzburg, Austria.
- Opening Hours: Daily from 9:30 AM to 5:00 PM (extended hours in summer).
- Ticket Prices: Adults €13.30, reduced rates for children, students, and seniors.
- Phone: +43 662 842 430 11

Hofburg Palace

Hofburg Palace in Vienna was the imperial winter residence of the Habsburg dynasty and is now a complex of museums and official residences.

Highlights:

Imperial Apartments: Tour the luxurious apartments of Emperor Franz Joseph and Empress Elisabeth (Sisi).

Sisi Museum: Delve into the fascinating life of Empress Elisabeth with exhibits of her personal belongings.

Imperial Silver Collection: Marvel at the exquisite collection of imperial tableware and ceremonial silver.

Practical Information:

- Location: Michaelerkuppel, 1010 Vienna, Austria.
- Opening Hours: Daily from 9:00 AM to 5:30 PM (hours may vary seasonally).
- Ticket Prices: Adults €15.00, reduced rates for children, students, and seniors.
- Phone: +43 1 533 75 70

Burg Kreuzenstein

Burg Kreuzenstein is a picturesque medieval castle located just north of Vienna. Rebuilt in the 19th century on the ruins of an original medieval fortress, it offers a glimpse into Austria's feudal past.

Highlights:

Castle Tour: Explore the well-preserved interiors, including the armory, chapel, and banquet hall.

Falconry Show: Watch an impressive falconry demonstration showcasing birds of prey in flight.

Scenic Views: Enjoy the beautiful views of the surrounding countryside and the Danube River.

Practical Information:

- Location: 2112 Leobendorf, Austria.
- Opening Hours: April to October, daily from 10:00 AM to 4:00 PM.
- Ticket Prices: Adults €13.00, reduced rates for children, students, and seniors.
- Phone: +43 2262 645 70

Burg Hohenwerfen

Burg Hohenwerfen is a stunning medieval fortress located high above the Salzach Valley in the Salzburg region.

Highlights:

Castle Tour: Discover the fortress's history through guided tours of its rooms, dungeons, and towers.

Falconry Center: Visit the falconry center and watch daily flight demonstrations.

Breathtaking Views: Take in the panoramic views of the surrounding mountains and valleys.

Practical Information:

- Location: Burgstraße 2, 5450 Werfen, Austria.
- Opening Hours: April to November, daily from 9:30 AM to 4:00 PM.
- Ticket Prices: Adults €13.00, reduced rates for children, students, and seniors.
- Phone: +43 6468 7603

Schloss Artstetten

Schloss Artstetten is a beautiful castle in Lower Austria, known for its connection to Archduke Franz Ferdinand, whose assassination sparked World War I.

Highlights:

Museum: Explore the museum dedicated to Franz Ferdinand and his family, featuring personal artifacts and historical exhibits.

Mausoleum: Visit the family mausoleum, where Franz Ferdinand and his wife, Sophie, are buried.

Gardens: Stroll through the lovely castle gardens, perfect for a relaxing afternoon.

Practical Information:

- Location: Schlossplatz 1, 3661 Artstetten, Austria.
- Opening Hours: April to November, daily from 9:00 AM to 5:00 PM.
- Ticket Prices: Adults €10.00, reduced rates for children, students, and seniors.
- Phone: +43 7413 8006

Schloss Ort

Schloss Ort is a picturesque castle located on an island in Lake Traunsee, in the heart of the Salzkammergut region.

Highlights:

Island Castle: Enjoy a scenic walk across the wooden bridge to the island castle.

Exhibitions: Visit the exhibitions showcasing local history and the castle's role in the region.

Lake Views: Take in the stunning views of Lake Traunsee and the surrounding mountains.

Practical Information:

- Location: Ort 1, 4810 Gmunden, Austria.
- Opening Hours: April to October, daily from 10:00 AM to 5:00 PM.
- Ticket Prices: Adults €6.00, reduced rates for children, students, and seniors.
- Phone: +43 7612 62499

Museums and Galleries

Kunsthistorisches Museum (Museum of Art History)

The Kunsthistorisches Museum in Vienna is one of the most important and largest art museums in the world. It houses an incredible collection of artworks from the Habsburg collections.

Highlights:

Old Masters Gallery: Featuring masterpieces by artists such as Titian, Rembrandt, Raphael, and Velázquez.

Egyptian and Near Eastern Collection: A fascinating collection of ancient artifacts, including mummies and sarcophagi.

Kunstkammer: An exquisite collection of Renaissance and Baroque art, including the famous Salt Cellar by Benvenuto Cellini.

Practical Information:

- Location: Maria-Theresien-Platz, 1010 Vienna, Austria.
- Opening Hours: Tuesday to Sunday from 10:00 AM to 6:00 PM, Thursday until 9:00 PM.
- Ticket Prices: Adults €18.00, reduced rates for children, students, and seniors.
- Phone: +43 1 525 24-0

Albertina

The Albertina in Vienna boasts one of the largest and most important print rooms in the world, along with a vast collection of modern art.

Highlights:

Graphic Collection: Featuring works by Dürer, Michelangelo, Rubens, and Klimt.

Modern Art Collection: Includes pieces by Picasso, Monet, and Chagall.

State Rooms: Explore the beautifully restored Habsburg staterooms.

Practical Information:

- Location: Albertinaplatz 1, 1010 Vienna, Austria.
- Opening Hours: Daily from 10:00 AM to 6:00 PM, Wednesday and Friday until 9:00 PM.
- Ticket Prices: Adults €17.90, reduced rates for children, students, and seniors.
- Phone: +43 1 534 83-0

Belvedere

The Belvedere in Vienna is a historic building complex that includes two Baroque palaces, the Upper and Lower Belvedere, housing a stunning art collection.

Highlights:

Klimt Collection: Home to the world's largest collection of works by Gustav Klimt, including "The Kiss."

Austrian Art: Extensive collections of Austrian art from the Middle Ages to the present day.

Baroque Gardens: Beautiful formal gardens connecting the Upper and Lower Belvedere.

Practical Information:

- Location: Prinz Eugen-Straße 27, 1030 Vienna, Austria.
- Opening Hours: Daily from 10:00 AM to 6:00 PM.
- Ticket Prices: Adults €16.50, reduced rates for children, students, and seniors.
- Phone: +43 1 795 57-0

Mumok (Museum Moderner Kunst Stiftung Ludwig Wien)

Mumok, located in the MuseumsQuartier in Vienna, is Austria's largest museum of modern and contemporary art.

Highlights:

Contemporary Art: Featuring works by Andy Warhol, Pablo Picasso, and Roy Lichtenstein.

Special Exhibitions: Regularly hosts innovative temporary exhibitions and installations.

Architectural Design: The museum's striking basalt stone exterior is a modern architectural highlight.

Practical Information:

- Location: Museumsplatz 1, 1070 Vienna, Austria.
- Opening Hours: Monday, Wednesday to Sunday from 10:00 AM to 6:00 PM, Thursday until 9:00 PM.
- Ticket Prices: Adults €12.00, reduced rates for children, students, and seniors.
- Phone: +43 1 525 00-0

Salzburg Museum

The Salzburg Museum provides a comprehensive look at the history, art, and culture of the city and region of Salzburg.

Highlights:

Panorama Museum: Features a 26-meter-long panorama painting of Salzburg by Johann Michael Sattler.

Art Collections: Displays fine and decorative arts from the Middle Ages to the 20th century.

Historical Exhibits: Learn about the history of Salzburg from its Roman roots to the present day.

Practical Information:

- Location: Mozartplatz 1, 5020 Salzburg, Austria.
- Opening Hours: Tuesday to Sunday from 9:00 AM to 5:00 PM.
- Ticket Prices: Adults €8.00, reduced rates for children, students, and seniors.
- Phone: +43 662 620 808-700

Kunsthaus Graz

Kunsthaus Graz, also known as the "Friendly Alien," is a contemporary art museum with a unique and futuristic architectural design.

Highlights:

Contemporary Exhibitions: Features cutting-edge contemporary art from international artists.

BIX Façade: The building's interactive facade, which lights up with changing displays.

Architectural Tour: Learn about the innovative design of the museum, created by architects Peter Cook and Colin Fournier.

Practical Information:

- Location: Lendkai 1, 8020 Graz, Austria.
- Opening Hours: Tuesday to Sunday from 10:00 AM to 6:00 PM.
- Ticket Prices: Adults €9.00, reduced rates for children, students, and seniors.
- Phone: +43 316 8017-9200

Schloss Ambras

Schloss Ambras in Innsbruck is a Renaissance castle and palace that houses a significant collection of art and armor.

Highlights:

Spanish Hall: One of the most beautiful Renaissance halls in the world, adorned with portraits of Tyrolean nobility.

Armory: An extensive collection of arms and armor, including pieces from the 15th and 16th centuries.

Portrait Gallery: Features portraits of the Habsburg rulers and other notable figures.

Practical Information:

- Location: Schloßstraße 20, 6020 Innsbruck, Austria.
- Opening Hours: Daily from 10:00 AM to 5:00 PM (hours may vary seasonally).
- Ticket Prices: Adults €12.00, reduced rates for children, students, and seniors.
- Phone: +43 1 525 24-4802

Historical Walking Tours

<u>Vienna: Imperial Grandeur and Hidden Gems</u>

Vienna, the capital city, is a treasure trove of history. A walking tour here will transport you back to the days of the Habsburg dynasty and beyond. Start your tour at the majestic Hofburg Palace, the former imperial residence. Stroll through the grand courtyards and visit the Imperial Apartments, where Emperor Franz Joseph and Empress Elisabeth once lived. Don't miss the stunning Spanish Riding School, where you can catch a glimpse of the world-famous Lipizzaner horses.

Next, head to St. Stephen's Cathedral, an iconic symbol of Vienna. Climb the 343 steps of the South Tower for a panoramic view of the city. Wander through the narrow, cobblestone streets of the old town, where you'll find hidden courtyards, quaint shops, and historic cafes. Make sure to stop at Café Central, a favorite haunt of famous figures like Sigmund Freud and Leon Trotsky.

End your tour at the MuseumsQuartier, one of the largest cultural complexes in the world. Here, you can explore the rich collections of the Kunsthistorisches Museum and the Leopold Museum. As you walk, Envision the lives of the composers, artists, and thinkers who once called Vienna home.

Practical Information:

- Tour Duration: Approximately 3-4 hours.
- Best Time to Visit: Spring and autumn for pleasant weather.
- Contact: Vienna Tourist Board, +43 1 24555

Salzburg: The Sound of Music and Medieval Majesty

Salzburg, the birthplace of Mozart and the setting for "The Sound of Music," is a city steeped in history and charm. Begin your walking tour at Mirabell Palace and Gardens, where scenes from the iconic film were shot. The beautifully manicured gardens offer a peaceful start to your day.

Cross the Salzach River via the Makartsteg bridge, adorned with thousands of love locks, and enter the old town. Here, you'll find the towering Hohensalzburg Fortress, one of the largest and best-preserved medieval castles in Europe. Take the funicular up to the fortress and explore its impressive halls, courtyards, and museums.

Stroll down Getreidegasse, Salzburg's most famous shopping street, lined with beautifully wrought iron signs and colorful buildings. Make sure to visit Mozart's Birthplace, now a museum dedicated to the composer's life and work. End your tour at Salzburg Cathedral, a baroque masterpiece with a stunning interior.

Practical Information:

- Tour Duration: Approximately 2-3 hours.
- Best Time to Visit: Summer for vibrant festivals and outdoor events.
- Contact: Salzburg Tourist Office, +43 662 88987-0

Graz: Renaissance Beauty and Modern Vibes

Graz, Austria's second-largest city, is a delightful blend of Renaissance elegance and modern innovation. Start your walking tour in the Hauptplatz, the city's main square, dominated by the impressive Town Hall. From here, wander through the historic old town, a UNESCO World Heritage site.

Make your way to the Landhaus, a stunning example of Renaissance architecture with its beautiful arcaded courtyard. Nearby, you'll find the Graz Cathedral and the Mausoleum of Emperor Ferdinand II, both must-see landmarks with rich histories.

Climb up to the Schlossberg, a hill in the center of Graz, where you can visit the iconic Clock Tower and enjoy panoramic views of the city. Descend via the Schlossbergstiege, a picturesque staircase that winds down the hill.

End your tour at the Kunsthaus Graz, affectionately known as the "Friendly Alien" for its unique design. This contemporary art museum contrasts beautifully with the historic buildings surrounding it and is a testament to Graz's dynamic cultural scene.

Practical Information:

- Tour Duration: Approximately 3 hours.
- Best Time to Visit: Late spring and early autumn for mild weather.

Innsbruck: Alpine Charm and Imperial Splendor

Innsbruck, nestled in the heart of the Alps, is known for its stunning mountain views and rich imperial history. Begin your walking tour at the Golden Roof, a famous landmark in the old town. The roof's gilded tiles shimmer in the sunlight, making it a perfect photo spot.

Next, visit the Hofkirche, home to the elaborate tomb of Emperor Maximilian I, surrounded by larger-than-life bronze statues. Just a short walk away is the Imperial Palace, where you can tour the luxurious state apartments and learn about the Habsburgs' influence on the region.

Stroll along Maria-Theresien-Straße, Innsbruck's main thoroughfare, lined with beautiful Baroque buildings and bustling with life. Stop by the Annasäule (St. Anne's Column) and enjoy the lively atmosphere of this vibrant street.

End your tour with a visit to the Bergisel Ski Jump, designed by Zaha Hadid. Take the funicular up to the observation deck for breathtaking views of the city and the surrounding mountains.

Practical Information:

- Tour Duration: Approximately 2-3 hours.
- Best Time to Visit: Winter for skiing and summer for hiking and outdoor activities.
- Contact: Innsbruck Information, +43 512 5356-0

Linz: Industrial Heritage and Cultural Revival

Linz, once known for its industrial might, has transformed into a vibrant cultural hub. Start your walking tour at the Hauptplatz, one of the largest squares in Europe, with the Trinity Column at its center. This bustling square is a great place to get a feel for the city's lively atmosphere.

Head towards the Ars Electronica Center, a museum dedicated to digital art and technology. Its interactive exhibits are fascinating for both adults and children. Cross the Nibelungen Bridge to the Lentos Art Museum, which houses an impressive collection of modern art.

Make your way to the Old Cathedral, with its beautiful baroque interior, and then climb up to the Pöstlingberg, a hill offering panoramic views of Linz. You can take the Pöstlingbergbahn, one of the steepest adhesion railways in Europe, to the top.

End your tour in the vibrant cultural quarter, where you can explore the OK Center for Contemporary Art and enjoy a meal at one of the many trendy restaurants.

Practical Information:

- Tour Duration: Approximately 3 hours.
- Best Time to Visit: Spring and autumn for mild weather.
- Contact: Linz Tourism, +43 732 7070-2009

WINE AND DINE

Austrian Cuisine Overview

Austrian cuisine is deeply rooted in the country's diverse geography and history. The culinary traditions here have been influenced by neighboring countries such as Germany, Hungary, Italy, and the former Austro-Hungarian Empire. This rich tapestry of flavors and techniques has resulted in a cuisine that's both comforting and sophisticated.

Austrian cooking often features hearty ingredients like potatoes, pork, beef, and dairy products. Fresh, locally sourced vegetables and fruits also play a significant role, along with herbs and spices that add depth to each dish. Bread, particularly dark rye and whole grain, is a staple at every meal.

Iconic Austrian Dishes

Wiener Schnitzel: This is perhaps Austria's most famous dish. A Wiener Schnitzel is a breaded and fried veal cutlet, typically served with a slice of lemon, potato salad, or lingonberry sauce. It's crispy on the outside, tender on the inside, and absolutely delicious.

Tafelspitz: A beloved traditional dish, Tafelspitz consists of boiled beef served with root vegetables, horseradish, and chive sauce. The meat is cooked to perfection, tender and flavorful, making it a favorite comfort food for many Austrians.

Gulasch: While originally from Hungary, goulash has become a staple in Austrian cuisine. Austrian Gulasch is a thick, hearty stew made with beef, onions, and paprika. It's often served with bread dumplings or potatoes, making it a perfect meal for cold weather.

Backhendl: This is Austria's take on fried chicken. The chicken is typically marinated, breaded, and then fried until golden and crispy. It's usually served with potato salad or a fresh garden salad.

Knödel: Dumplings, or Knödel, are a versatile and popular side dish. They come in various forms, such as Semmelknödel (bread dumplings), Kartoffelknödel (potato dumplings), and Leberknödel (liver dumplings). These are often served with rich sauces or as accompaniments to meats.

Käsespätzle: Think of this as Austria's version of mac and cheese. Käsespätzle is a dish of soft egg noodles layered with melted cheese and topped with crispy onions. It's hearty, cheesy, and incredibly satisfying.

Austrian Pastries and Desserts

Austria is renowned for its pastries and desserts, many of which are enjoyed in the country's famous coffeehouses.

Apfelstrudel: Apple strudel is a classic Austrian dessert made with thin, flaky pastry filled with spiced apples, raisins, and breadcrumbs. It's often served warm, dusted with powdered sugar, and sometimes accompanied by a dollop of whipped cream.

Sachertorte: This is a rich chocolate cake that originated at the Hotel Sacher in Vienna. The cake is layered with apricot jam and covered in a smooth chocolate glaze. It's usually served with a side of unsweetened whipped cream.

Kaiserschmarrn: A favorite for both dessert and breakfast, Kaiserschmarrn is a fluffy, shredded pancake served with powdered sugar and fruit compote. The name translates to "Emperor's Mess," and it's as delightful to eat as it is to say.

Linzer Torte: Known as the world's oldest cake recipe, Linzer Torte is a nutty, buttery pastry filled with raspberry or red currant jam and topped with a lattice crust. It's named after the city of Linz and is a must-try for pastry lovers.

Austrian Beverages

No overview of Austrian cuisine would be complete without mentioning the beverages that complement the food.

Coffee: Austria has a rich coffeehouse culture, with Viennese coffeehouses being world-famous. Popular coffee variations include the Melange (similar to a cappuccino), Einspänner (strong black coffee topped with whipped cream), and Verlängerter (a longer, milder black coffee).

Wine: Austria produces excellent wines, particularly white wines such as Grüner Veltliner and Riesling. The wine regions of Wachau, Burgenland, and Styria are known for their high-quality vineyards and picturesque landscapes.

Beer: Austrian beers, especially lagers and Märzen, are widely enjoyed. The country has a long tradition of brewing, with many regional breweries offering distinctive flavors.

Schnapps: A traditional fruit brandy, schnapps is often made from apricots, pears, or plums. It's commonly enjoyed as a digestif after meals.

Top Restaurants across Austria

Recommended Restaurants in Vienna

Amador

Experience the pinnacle of fine dining at Vienna's only three-Michelin-starred restaurant, Amador. Chef Juan Amador's kitchen is renowned for its creative and innovative dishes that blend Spanish roots with

Austrian ingredients. The dining room's open-plan design allows diners to watch the culinary magic unfold.

- Price: Blowout
- Opening Hours: Wednesday to Saturday, 6:30 PM - 9:00 PM
- Phone: +43 660 90 75 991
- Address: Grinzinger Straße 86, 1190 Vienna, Austria
- Rating: 5 stars

Steirereck

Nestled in the serene Stadtpark, Steirereck offers a two-Michelin-star dining experience with an emphasis on contemporary Austrian cuisine. Chef Heinz Reitbauer's innovative dishes utilize herbs grown on the restaurant's rooftop.

- Price: Blowout
- Opening Hours: Monday to Friday, 11:30 AM - 3:00 PM, 6:30 PM - 11:00 PM
- Phone: +43 1 713 31 68
- Address: Am Heumarkt 2A, 1030 Vienna, Austria
- Rating: 5 stars

Konstantin Filippou

Chef Konstantin Filippou's Michelin-starred restaurant offers a fusion of Mediterranean flavors and Austrian ingredients. The minimalist, elegant interior complements the refined dishes served in multi-course menus.

- Price: Blowout
- Opening Hours: Tuesday to Saturday, 12:00 PM - 3:00 PM, 6:30 PM - 10:30 PM
- Phone: +43 1 512 22 29
- Address: Dominikanerbastei 17, 1010 Vienna, Austria
- Rating: 5 stars

Recommended Restaurants in Salzburg

Restaurant Ikarus

Located in the iconic Hangar-7, Restaurant Ikarus features a rotating roster of guest chefs from around the world, curated by Eckart Witzigmann. The innovative menu changes monthly, offering a unique dining experience every time.

- Price: Blowout
- Opening Hours: Monday to Saturday, 7:00 PM - 11:00 PM
- Phone: +43 662 2197 77
- Address: Wilhelm-Spazier-Straße 7A, 5020 Salzburg, Austria
- Rating: 5 stars

St. Peter Stiftskeller

Known as the oldest restaurant in Europe, St. Peter Stiftskeller offers a historic dining experience with traditional Austrian cuisine. The candlelit dining rooms and classical music performances enhance the ambiance.

- Price: Pricey
- Opening Hours: Daily, 11:30 AM - 11:00 PM
- Phone: +43 662 841 268
- Address: St. Peter Bezirk 1/4, 5020 Salzburg, Austria
- Rating: 5 stars

Triangel

A favorite among locals, Triangel serves up hearty Austrian dishes with a focus on fresh, regional ingredients. The cozy atmosphere and friendly service make it a perfect spot for a relaxed meal.

- Price: Moderate
- Opening Hours: Daily, 11:30 AM - 11:00 PM
- Phone: +43 662 84 50 50

- Address: Wiener-Philharmoniker-Gasse 7, 5020 Salzburg, Austria
- Rating: 4.5 stars

Recommended Restaurants in Innsbruck

Schaufelspitz

Located at the top of the Stubai Glacier, Schaufelspitz combines breathtaking views with gourmet alpine cuisine. The restaurant's modern dishes are crafted from local ingredients and served with a spectacular mountain backdrop.

- Price: Pricey
- Opening Hours: Daily, 11:30 AM - 3:30 PM
- Phone: +43 5226 8141 324
- Address: Mutterberg 2, 6167 Neustift im Stubaital, Austria
- Rating: 5 stars

Die Wilderin

Die Wilderin prides itself on using sustainably sourced, seasonal ingredients. The menu changes frequently to reflect what's fresh and available, and the dishes are prepared with creativity and care.

- Price: Moderate
- Opening Hours: Tuesday to Saturday, 6:00 PM - 11:00 PM
- Phone: +43 512 562 728
- Address: Seilergasse 5, 6020 Innsbruck, Austria
- Rating: 4.5 stars

Lichtblick

Situated on the top floor of a modern building, Lichtblick offers panoramic views of Innsbruck alongside its innovative cuisine. The menu blends traditional Austrian flavors with modern techniques.

- Price: Pricey

- Opening Hours: Monday to Saturday, 12:00 PM - 2:00 PM, 6:00 PM - 10:00 PM
- Phone: +43 512 56 31 71
- Address: Maria-Theresien-Straße 18, 6020 Innsbruck, Austria
- Rating: 5 stars

Recommended Restaurants in Graz

Schlossberg Restaurant

Perched atop the Schlossberg hill, this restaurant offers stunning views of Graz and an elegant dining experience. The menu features refined Austrian and international dishes, beautifully presented.

- Price: Pricey
- Opening Hours: Daily, 12:00 PM - 3:00 PM, 6:00 PM - 11:00 PM
- Phone: +43 316 84 24 00
- Address: Schlossberg 7, 8010 Graz, Austria
- Rating: 5 stars

Der Steirer

A beloved spot for Styrian cuisine, Der Steirer offers traditional dishes with a modern twist. The lively atmosphere and excellent wine list make it a great place to sample local flavors.

- Price: Moderate
- Opening Hours: Monday to Saturday, 11:00 AM - 12:00 AM
- Phone: +43 316 70 36 54
- Address: Belgiergasse 1, 8020 Graz, Austria
- Rating: 4.5 stars

Aiola Upstairs

Located in the heart of Graz, Aiola Upstairs provides a chic setting with innovative cuisine. The stylish interior and creative menu make it a popular choice for both locals and visitors.

- Price: Pricey
- Opening Hours: Monday to Saturday, 11:00 AM - 2:00 AM
- Phone: +43 316 81 86 77
- Address: Schlossberg 2, 8010 Graz, Austria
- Rating: 5 stars

Wine Regions and Tours

Wachau

The Wachau Valley, a UNESCO World Heritage site, is renowned for its terraced vineyards along the Danube River. Known for producing world-class Grüner Veltliner and Riesling, the region's wines are celebrated for their elegance and complexity.

- Top Wineries: Domäne Wachau, Nikolaihof, and Weingut Emmerich Knoll.
- Tour Highlights: River cruises, scenic bike rides through vineyards, and wine tastings in historic cellars.

Burgenland

Burgenland, located in eastern Austria, is famous for its full-bodied red wines, particularly Blaufränkisch, as well as dessert wines like Ruster Ausbruch. The region's Pannonian climate provides ideal conditions for diverse wine styles.

- Top Wineries: Weingut Ernst Triebaumer, Weingut Moric, and Weingut Kracher.
- Tour Highlights: Visits to Lake Neusiedl, exploring historic towns like Rust, and sampling unique dessert wines.

Styria (Steiermark)

Styria, often referred to as the "Tuscany of Austria," is known for its aromatic white wines, especially Sauvignon Blanc, and picturesque rolling hills. The region's wines are vibrant and fresh, reflecting the terroir.

- Top Wineries: Weingut Tement, Weingut Sattlerhof, and Weingut Gross.
- Tour Highlights: Wine routes with breathtaking views, gourmet food pairings, and visiting charming wine taverns (Buschenschank).

Lower Austria (Niederösterreich)

Lower Austria encompasses several important sub-regions such as Kamptal, Kremstal, and the Thermenregion. The area is known for its diverse wine styles, including crisp Grüner Veltliners and aromatic Rieslings.

- Top Wineries: Weingut Bründlmayer, Weingut Schloss Gobelsburg, and Weingut Nigl.
- Tour Highlights: Exploring historic wine towns, guided vineyard walks, and attending wine festivals.

Recommended Wine Tours

Wachau Wine Experience Tour

Discover the beauty of the Wachau Valley with a guided tour that includes wine tastings, a Danube River cruise, and visits to charming towns like Dürnstein. Sample some of the region's best wines and learn about the local viticulture.

- Price: Approximately €150 per person.
- Duration: Full day.
- Contact: Wachau Wine Tours, +43 2712 30201
- Rating: 5 stars

Burgenland Red Wine Tour

Explore the rich red wines of Burgenland with visits to top wineries, including tastings of Blaufränkisch and St. Laurent. Enjoy scenic drives around Lake Neusiedl and experience the region's unique winemaking traditions.

- Price: Approximately €130 per person.
- Duration: Full day.
- Contact: Burgenland Wine Tours, +43 2682 77511
- Rating: 5 stars

Styrian Wine Road Tour

Travel through the stunning landscapes of Styria, stopping at premier wineries to taste Sauvignon Blanc, Muskateller, and other regional specialties. The tour includes gourmet food pairings and visits to local Buschenschank.

- Price: Approximately €140 per person.
- Duration: Full day.
- Contact: Styrian Wine Roads, +43 3453 70522
- Rating: 5 stars

Lower Austria Wine Trail

Embark on a journey through the diverse wine regions of Lower Austria. The tour includes tastings at prestigious wineries, visits to historical sites, and the opportunity to meet winemakers.

- Price: Approximately €135 per person.
- Duration: Full day.
- Phone: +43 2732 70434
- Rating: 5 stars

FESTIVALS AND EVENTS

Major Annual Festivals

Vienna Opera Ball

The Vienna Opera Ball, held annually in February, is the epitome of Viennese elegance and tradition. Taking place at the opulent Vienna State Opera, this glamorous event transforms the opera house into a grand ballroom. The ball opens with a procession of debutantes and their escorts, dressed in stunning white gowns and black tails, followed by a magnificent dance performance.

Visitors can expect an evening of classical music, waltzing, and high fashion. It's a night where the elite of society gather, but it's also accessible to those who wish to experience the grandeur of a traditional Viennese ball. The atmosphere is electric, with live orchestras playing waltzes, polkas, and operatic arias. Attending the Vienna Opera Ball is like stepping back in time to a world of aristocratic splendor.

- When: February
- Where: Vienna State Opera, Vienna

Salzburg Festival

The Salzburg Festival, held every summer from late July to August, is one of the most prestigious music and drama festivals in the world. Founded in 1920, it celebrates classical music, opera, and theater. The festival takes place in various historic venues throughout Salzburg, including the Felsenreitschule and the Großes Festspielhaus.

What makes the Salzburg Festival unique is its rich history and the quality of its performances. Visitors can expect to see world-class productions featuring renowned conductors, soloists, and orchestras.

The festival's program includes a mix of classical operas, contemporary works, and dramatic plays. It's a cultural feast for any art lover and a testament to Salzburg's legacy as the birthplace of Mozart.

- When: Late July to August
- Where: Various venues, Salzburg

Viennale

The Viennale, Vienna's international film festival, takes place every October and is a highlight for cinephiles. Over two weeks, the festival screens a diverse selection of international films, including feature films, documentaries, and short films. Screenings are held in some of Vienna's most iconic cinemas, such as the Gartenbaukino and the Urania.

The Viennale is unique for its eclectic and inclusive program, which often features films that challenge mainstream cinema conventions. Visitors can expect to see innovative films from both established and emerging directors. The festival also hosts discussions, panels, and retrospectives, offering a deeper insight into the world of cinema. It's a vibrant, intellectually stimulating event that attracts filmmakers and film enthusiasts from around the globe.

- When: October
- Where: Various cinemas, Vienna

Innsbruck Christmas Market

The Innsbruck Christmas Market, held from mid-November to early January, is one of the most enchanting holiday experiences in Austria. Set against the backdrop of the snow-capped Alps, the market is spread across several locations in Innsbruck, including the Old Town and Maria-Theresien-Strasse.

Visitors can expect a festive atmosphere filled with twinkling lights, the aroma of mulled wine and roasted chestnuts, and the sound of Christmas carols. The market features a variety of stalls selling handmade crafts, decorations, and traditional Tyrolean food. A highlight is the towering Christmas tree in front of the Golden Roof, a historic landmark. The Innsbruck Christmas Market is a magical experience for all ages, capturing the spirit of the holiday season.

- When: Mid-November to early January
- Where: Various locations, Innsbruck

Steirischer Herbst

Steirischer Herbst, or Styrian Autumn, is an avant-garde arts festival held in Graz every September and October. The festival is known for its cutting-edge performances, exhibitions, and installations that push the boundaries of contemporary art. It includes a wide range of artistic disciplines, from visual arts and theater to music and literature.

What makes Steirischer Herbst unique is its focus on experimental and provocative art that often addresses social and political issues. Visitors can expect to see groundbreaking works from international artists, thought-provoking discussions, and immersive experiences. It's a festival that challenges perceptions and inspires creativity, making it a must-attend for contemporary art enthusiasts.

- When: September to October
- Where: Various venues, Graz

Local Celebrations

Krampusnacht (Krampus Night)

Krampusnacht is a fascinating and somewhat eerie celebration that takes place on the evening of December 5th, the night before St. Nicholas Day. This tradition is particularly strong in the Alpine regions of Austria.

Krampus, a fearsome creature with horns, fangs, and a long tongue, is said to accompany St. Nicholas. While St. Nicholas rewards well-behaved children with gifts, Krampus is believed to punish those who have been naughty. The celebration includes parades where people dress up as Krampus, donning elaborate costumes and masks.

Krampusnacht is a blend of pagan and Christian traditions, offering a thrilling experience with its parades and performances. The celebrations are often accompanied by bonfires, music, and festive markets.

- Date: December 5th
- Locations: Primarily in the Alpine regions, such as Salzburg, Tyrol, and Styria.

What to Expect:

Visitors can expect to see Krampus processions (Krampusläufe) with participants wearing intricately designed costumes and masks. The atmosphere is both festive and spooky, making it a unique cultural experience.

Almabtrieb (Cattle Drive)

Almabtrieb, or the Alpine cattle drive, is a traditional celebration marking the end of the summer grazing season. Farmers bring their cattle down from the mountain pastures to the valleys, and the event is celebrated with great fanfare.

Cattle are adorned with colorful garlands, flowers, and bells as they are herded through villages. The celebration honors the safe return of the animals and the successful grazing season.

Almabtrieb showcases the close connection between Austrian farmers and their livestock. It's a vibrant and picturesque event that reflects rural life and traditions.

- Date: Late September to early October
- Locations: Various alpine regions, including Tyrol, Salzburg, and Vorarlberg.

What to Expect:

Expect to see beautifully decorated cattle paraded through towns, accompanied by traditional music, dancing, and markets selling local crafts and food.

Fasching (Carnival)

Fasching, or Carnival, is a lively and colorful celebration that takes place in the weeks leading up to Lent. It's a time of parties, parades, and elaborate costumes, with each region adding its unique flavor to the festivities.

Fasching is characterized by costume balls, street parades, and various events that bring communities together to celebrate before the fasting period of Lent.

Each region has its traditions and specialties. In Vienna, the highlight is the famous Opera Ball, while smaller towns might have local parades and masquerade balls.

- Date: Varies each year, ending on Shrove Tuesday (the day before Ash Wednesday).
- Locations: Nationwide, with major celebrations in Vienna, Salzburg, and Villach.

What to Expect:

Visitors can expect vibrant parades, lively music, and people in elaborate costumes. Many towns have specific events, like the Villach Carnival with its humorous speeches and performances.

Perchtenlauf (Perchten Processions)

Perchtenlauf is a traditional winter festival featuring the Perchten, mythical creatures that are said to drive away evil spirits and bring good fortune for the new year. This celebration is particularly strong in the Salzburg region.

The Perchten are divided into two groups: the Schönperchten (beautiful Perchten) and the Schiachperchten (ugly Perchten). The processions include people dressed as these creatures, with elaborate masks and costumes.

Perchtenlauf is deeply rooted in pagan traditions and offers a fascinating glimpse into ancient customs. The masks and costumes are works of art, crafted with intricate details.

- Date: Early January, often coinciding with Epiphany (January 6th).
- Locations: Salzburg and surrounding areas.

What to Expect:

Expect to see processions with people dressed as Perchten, accompanied by music and dancing. The atmosphere is both festive and mysterious, with a strong sense of tradition.

Steirisches Kürbisfest (Styrian Pumpkin Festival)

The Styrian Pumpkin Festival celebrates the harvest of pumpkins, a staple in the region known for its pumpkin seed oil. The festival is a fun and family-friendly event that highlights the culinary and cultural significance of pumpkins in Styria.

The festival includes pumpkin carving competitions, culinary demonstrations, and markets selling pumpkin-based products. It's a celebration of the autumn harvest and local agriculture.

Styria is renowned for its pumpkin seed oil, and the festival showcases this regional specialty. Visitors can sample various pumpkin dishes and buy products to take home.

- Date: Early October
- Locations: Various towns in Styria, particularly around the town of Feldbach.

What to Expect:

Visitors can expect a colorful display of pumpkins, from giant gourds to intricately carved masterpieces. The festival includes food stalls, live music, and activities for children.

Music and Arts Festivals

Salzburg Festival

The Salzburg Festival is one of the world's most prestigious and well-known festivals, dedicated to classical music, opera, and drama. Held every summer in Salzburg, the birthplace of Mozart, the festival attracts top artists and audiences from around the globe.

The festival is famous for its high-caliber performances and the stunning historical venues in which they take place, such as the Felsenreitschule and the Großes Festspielhaus. It celebrates the works of Mozart, as well as other classical and contemporary composers, offering a rich program that includes operas, concerts, and plays.

- Date: Late July to August

- Location: Salzburg

What to Expect:

Visitors can expect world-class performances by leading orchestras, conductors, and soloists. The festival's program includes both classic works and innovative productions, providing a diverse and enriching experience.

Vienna Festival (Wiener Festwochen)

The Vienna Festival is a celebration of performing arts, featuring theater, dance, music, and visual arts from around the world. Held annually in Vienna, the festival transforms the city into a vibrant cultural hub for several weeks.

The festival is known for its innovative and boundary-pushing performances, often featuring avant-garde and experimental works. It brings together artists and audiences from diverse cultural backgrounds, fostering a global dialogue through the arts.

- Date: May to June
- Location: Various venues, Vienna

What to Expect:

Expect a dynamic mix of performances, including international theater productions, contemporary dance, and experimental music. The festival also includes workshops, discussions, and exhibitions, offering a comprehensive cultural experience.

Bregenz Festival

The Bregenz Festival is famous for its spectacular opera performances on a floating stage on Lake Constance. This unique setting, combined with world-class productions, makes the festival a must-visit for opera lovers.

The floating stage, with its stunning backdrops and innovative stage designs, creates an unforgettable visual and auditory experience. The festival's productions often incorporate modern technology and artistic elements, enhancing the traditional opera format.

- Date: July to August
- Location: Bregenz, Lake Constance

What to Expect:

Visitors can expect grand opera productions featuring elaborate sets and costumes, as well as performances by leading international opera singers and orchestras. The festival also includes orchestral concerts and theater performances.

Ars Electronica Festival

The Ars Electronica Festival in Linz is a pioneering event that explores the intersection of art, technology, and society. It brings together artists, scientists, and technologists to showcase cutting-edge works and innovations.

The festival is renowned for its forward-thinking approach and its ability to bridge the gap between art and technology. It features interactive installations, digital art, performances, and discussions that challenge conventional boundaries and explore future possibilities.

- Date: September
- Location: Linz

What to Expect:

Expect to see groundbreaking digital art, robotics, AI projects, and immersive installations. The festival also includes symposiums, workshops, and presentations by leading thinkers and innovators.

ImPulsTanz Vienna International Dance Festival

ImPulsTanz is one of Europe's largest contemporary dance festivals, attracting dancers and choreographers from around the world. Held in Vienna, the festival offers performances, workshops, and residencies.

The festival is known for its diverse and innovative dance performances, ranging from classical ballet to contemporary and experimental dance. It provides a platform for both established and emerging artists to showcase their work.

- Date: July to August
- Location: Various venues, Vienna

What to Expect:

Visitors can expect an exciting program of dance performances, workshops, and masterclasses. The festival also includes discussions and film screenings related to dance and movement.

ACCOMMODATION OPTIONS

Hotels and Resorts

Top Hotels and Resorts in Vienna

Hotel Sacher Wien

Hotel Sacher Wien is an iconic luxury hotel located in the heart of Vienna, directly opposite the Vienna State Opera. Founded in 1876, it has a rich history and has hosted numerous celebrities and dignitaries over the years. The hotel combines old-world charm with modern amenities, featuring elegantly decorated rooms and suites, a renowned spa, and gourmet dining options including the famous Café Sacher, where you can indulge in the original Sachertorte.

- Price: From €600 per night
- Phone: +43 1 514560
- Address: Philharmoniker Str. 4, 1010 Vienna, Austria
- Rating: 5 stars

The Ritz-Carlton, Vienna

The Ritz-Carlton, Vienna blends historic charm with contemporary luxury. Located on the iconic Ring Boulevard, this five-star hotel is housed in four historic palaces. The rooms and suites are designed with a mix of modern and traditional decor, offering stunning views of the city. The hotel features a luxurious spa, a rooftop bar with panoramic views, and several dining options including the elegant Dstrikt Steakhouse.

- Price: From €450 per night
- Phone: +43 1 31188
- Address: Schubertring 5-7, 1010 Vienna, Austria
- Rating: 5 stars

Park Hyatt Vienna

Located in a former bank building, Park Hyatt Vienna is a luxurious hotel that seamlessly combines historical elegance with modern luxury. Situated in the city's Golden Quarter, it offers spacious rooms and suites with high ceilings and lavish furnishings. The hotel features a spa with an indoor swimming pool, a fitness center, and several dining options including the stylish The Bank Brasserie & Bar.

- Price: From €550 per night
- Phone: +43 1 22740
- Address: Am Hof 2, 1010 Vienna, Austria
- Rating: 5 stars

Top Hotels and Resorts in Salzburg

Hotel Sacher Salzburg

Hotel Sacher Salzburg is a luxurious five-star hotel that perfectly combines historic charm with modern amenities. Located on the banks of the Salzach River, it offers stunning views of the old town and the Hohensalzburg Fortress. The rooms are elegantly decorated, reflecting the hotel's rich history. Guests can enjoy world-class dining at the hotel's restaurants, including the renowned Café Sacher, famous for its original Sachertorte.

- Price: From €450 per night
- Phone: +43 662 889770
- Address: Schwarzstraße 5-7, 5020 Salzburg, Austria
- Rating: 5 stars

Hotel Goldener Hirsch, a Luxury Collection Hotel

Hotel Goldener Hirsch is a historic hotel located on Getreidegasse, one of Salzburg's most famous streets. This five-star property offers a blend of traditional Austrian décor with modern comforts. Each room is uniquely decorated with antique furniture, luxurious fabrics, and original artwork. The hotel is known for its exceptional service and its restaurant, which serves gourmet Austrian cuisine.

- Price: From €400 per night
- Phone: +43 662 80840
- Address: Getreidegasse 37, 5020 Salzburg, Austria
- Rating: 5 stars

Schloss Mönchstein Hotel

Perched on top of Mönchsberg Mountain, Schloss Mönchstein Hotel offers breathtaking views over Salzburg. This five-star luxury hotel is set in a historic castle, providing a unique and romantic setting. The rooms and suites are lavishly decorated, and the hotel features a spa, an outdoor pool, and a gourmet restaurant, "The Glass Garden," which offers panoramic views of the city.

- Price: From €600 per night
- Phone: +43 662 848555
- Address: Mönchsberg Park 26, 5020 Salzburg, Austria
- Rating: 5 stars

Top Hotels and Resorts in Innsbruck

Adlers Hotel

Adlers Hotel is known for its contemporary design and breathtaking panoramic views of the Alps. Located in the heart of Innsbruck, this stylish hotel features modern rooms with floor-to-ceiling windows, a rooftop bar, and a restaurant offering gourmet cuisine. The hotel is also conveniently close to major attractions, making it an ideal base for exploring the city.

- Price: From €180 per night
- Phone: +43 512 56 31 00
- Address: Brunecker Str. 1, 6020 Innsbruck, Austria
- Rating: 4.5 stars

Grand Hotel Europa

Grand Hotel Europa is a historic hotel that combines traditional Tyrolean charm with modern luxury. Located near the train station, it offers easy access to both the city center and the surrounding mountains. The hotel features elegantly decorated rooms, a renowned restaurant serving regional specialties, and a cozy bar.

- Price: From €200 per night
- Phone: +43 512 59310
- Address: Südtiroler Pl. 2, 6020 Innsbruck, Austria
- Rating: 5 stars

NALA Individuellhotel

NALA Individuellhotel offers a unique and artistic experience in Innsbruck. Each room in this boutique hotel is individually designed with creative and modern décor. Located close to the old town, it provides easy access to local attractions and cultural sites. The hotel also features a beautiful garden, a fitness center, and a cozy café.

- Price: From €150 per night
- Phone: +43 512 58 38 88
- Address: Müllerstraße 15, 6020 Innsbruck, Austria
- Rating: 4.5 stars

Top Hotels and Resorts in Graz

Schlossberghotel – Das Kunsthotel

Schlossberghotel – Das Kunsthotel is an elegant hotel located at the foot of the Schlossberg hill. This boutique hotel is adorned with a unique collection of contemporary art, creating a sophisticated yet welcoming atmosphere. The rooms are individually decorated with a blend of modern amenities and classic charm. Guests can enjoy the rooftop terrace with stunning views over Graz, a serene garden, and an outdoor pool.

- Price: From €220 per night
- Phone: +43 316 80 76 0
- Address: Kaiser-Franz-Josef-Kai 30, 8010 Graz, Austria
- Rating: 5 stars

Parkhotel Graz

Parkhotel Graz offers traditional luxury with modern comforts. Located in the historic city center, this four-star hotel features stylish rooms, a beautiful garden, and an excellent wellness area. The on-site restaurant serves exquisite Austrian cuisine, and the cozy bar is perfect for relaxing with a drink.

- Price: From €180 per night
- Phone: +43 316 32 13 21
- Address: Leonhardstraße 8, 8010 Graz, Austria
- Rating: 4.5 stars

Grand Hôtel Wiesler

Grand Hôtel Wiesler is a historic hotel that blends classic and contemporary styles. Located along the Mur River, it offers easy access to Graz's major attractions. The hotel features modern rooms, a fitness center, and a trendy restaurant, "Speisesaal," which offers an innovative menu with international and Austrian dishes.

- Price: From €200 per night
- Phone: +43 316 70 66
- Address: Grieskai 4-8, 8020 Graz, Austria
- Rating: 5 stars

Budget Lodging

Top Budget Lodging in Vienna

Hotel Lucia

Hotel Lucia offers a comfortable and affordable stay in Vienna, just a short walk from the city center. This family-run hotel features modern rooms with cozy furnishings, making it a perfect home base for exploring the city. Guests can enjoy a generous breakfast buffet each morning and the friendly staff is always ready to assist with tips and recommendations.

- Price: From €80 per night
- Phone: +43 1 982 11 02
- Address: Hütteldorfer Str. 79, 1150 Vienna, Austria
- Rating: 4.5 stars

JUFA Hotel Wien City

JUFA Hotel Wien City is a great choice for budget-conscious travelers looking for modern amenities and a convenient location. Situated in the Simmering district, the hotel offers easy access to the city center and major attractions. The spacious rooms are perfect for families, and the hotel features a restaurant, bar, and play area for children.

- Price: From €90 per night
- Phone: +43 1 740 75 020
- Address: Mautner-Markhof-Gasse 50, 1110 Vienna, Austria
- Rating: 4.5 stars

Motel One Wien-Hauptbahnhof

Motel One Wien-Hauptbahnhof offers stylish and affordable accommodation right next to Vienna's main train station. This modern hotel features chic, well-designed rooms with comfortable beds and free WiFi. Guests can enjoy a hearty breakfast and unwind in the trendy lounge area.

- Price: From €85 per night
- Phone: +43 1 6020000

- Address: Gerhard-Bronner-Straße 11, 1100 Vienna, Austria
- Rating: 4.5 stars

Top Budget Lodging in Salzburg

Motel One Salzburg-Mirabell

Motel One Salzburg-Mirabell is a modern budget hotel situated along the riverfront, providing a scenic and peaceful environment. The hotel offers comfortable rooms with contemporary decor, air conditioning, and free WiFi. It's about a 15-minute walk from both the old town and the main train station, making it a convenient location for exploring Salzburg.

- Price: From €85 per night
- Phone: +43 662 885200
- Address: Elisabethkai 58-60, 5020 Salzburg, Austria
- Rating: 4.5 stars

Hotel Hofwirt Salzburg

Hotel Hofwirt Salzburg is a charming and affordable hotel located just a short walk from the main attractions of the old town. The hotel features comfortable rooms, a complimentary breakfast buffet, and free WiFi throughout the property. It combines traditional Austrian hospitality with modern amenities, ensuring a comfortable stay.

- Price: From €90 per night
- Phone: +43 662 8721720
- Address: Schallmooser Hauptstraße 1, 5020 Salzburg, Austria
- Rating: 4.5 stars

Adlerhof

Adlerhof is a family-run budget hotel located near Salzburg's main train station, making it an excellent base for travelers. The hotel offers simple yet comfortable rooms, free breakfast, and free WiFi. Its location is convenient for accessing public transportation and exploring the city's main sights.

- Price: From €80 per night
- Phone: +43 662 875236
- Address: Elisabethstraße 25, 5020 Salzburg, Austria
- Rating: 4.5 stars

Top Budget Lodging in Innsbruck

Hotel Kapeller Innsbruck

Hotel Kapeller Innsbruck is a comfortable and modern budget hotel located in the quiet district of Amras, just a short tram ride from the city center. The hotel features spacious rooms with contemporary furnishings, free WiFi, and complimentary breakfast. Guests can enjoy the serene atmosphere and easy access to the city's attractions.

- Price: From €100 per night
- Phone: +43 512 344333
- Address: Philippine-Welser-Straße 96, 6020 Innsbruck, Austria
- Rating: 4.5 stars

Weisses Rössl

Weisses Rössl is a charming budget hotel located in the heart of Innsbruck's old town. This historic hotel offers cozy rooms, some with beautiful views of the city. Guests can enjoy a complimentary breakfast and free WiFi, as well as easy access to many of Innsbruck's cultural landmarks and attractions.

- Price: From €90 per night
- Phone: +43 512 583057
- Address: Kiebachgasse 8, 6020 Innsbruck, Austria
- Rating: 4.5 stars

Pension Stoi Budget Guesthouse

Pension Stoi Budget Guesthouse is a simple yet popular guesthouse situated in the city center, close to the main train station. The guesthouse offers basic but comfortable rooms, free WiFi, and a relaxed atmosphere. It's a great option for travelers looking for affordable accommodation without sacrificing convenience.

- Price: From €80 per night
- Phone: +43 512 587492
- Address: Salurner Straße 7, 6020 Innsbruck, Austria
- Rating: 3.5 stars

Top Budget Lodging in Graz

Hotel Feichtinger Graz

Hotel Feichtinger Graz offers modern and comfortable rooms at an affordable price. Located close to the Mur River and within walking distance of the old town, this hotel provides easy access to many of Graz's main attractions. The rooms are spacious and well-equipped, with amenities such as free WiFi and flat-screen TVs. Guests can enjoy a generous breakfast buffet each morning.

- Price: From €85 per night
- Phone: +43 316 720720
- Address: Lendplatz 1a, 8020 Graz, Austria
- Rating: 4.5 stars

Ibis Budget Graz City

Ibis Budget Graz City offers simple yet comfortable accommodations at a very reasonable price. Located just a short walk from the Graz city center, this hotel provides easy access to public transportation and local attractions. The rooms are modern and efficient, featuring free WiFi and satellite TV. A vending machine is available for snacks and drinks.

- Price: From €70 per night
- Phone: +43 316 764400
- Address: Neubaugasse 11, 8020 Graz, Austria
- Rating: 3.5 stars

Unique Stays

Unique Stays in Vienna

Hotel König von Ungarn

Hotel König von Ungarn is the oldest hotel in Vienna, dating back to 1746. It is located in the heart of the city, just a short walk from St. Stephen's Cathedral. The hotel combines historical charm with modern comfort, featuring quirky wallpapers, classic decor, and a lobby with an indoor garden.

- Price: From €150 per night
- Phone: +43 1 515840
- Address: Schulerstraße 10, 1010 Vienna, Austria
- Website: Rating: 5 stars

Magdas Hotel

Magdas Hotel is a social business hotel created by the charity organization Caritas. Located near the Prater Park, this hotel employs refugees and offers creatively upcycled interiors. Each room has its own unique design, and some provide views of the iconic Riesenrad (Ferris wheel). The hotel's mission and innovative decor make it a standout choice for socially conscious travelers.

- Price: From €100 per night
- Phone: +43 1 7200288
- Address: Laufbergergasse 12, 1020 Vienna, Austria
- Rating: 4.5 stars

Hotel Altstadt Vienna

Hotel Altstadt Vienna is a minimalist boutique hotel located in the vibrant Neubau district. It features an extensive collection of contemporary art and offers a serene and stylish stay. Guests can enjoy a delicious breakfast buffet with locally sourced ingredients and unwind in the hotel bar or in front of the open fireplace.

- Price: From €120 per night
- Phone: +43 1 5226666
- Address: Kirchengasse 41, 1070 Vienna, Austria
- Rating: 5 stars

Unique Stays in Salzburg

Hotel Stein

Hotel Stein offers a blend of historical architecture and modern design, located along the Salzach River with stunning views of the old town and the Hohensalzburg Fortress. The hotel features contemporary rooms and a rooftop bar that provides panoramic views of Salzburg.

- Price: From €160 per night
- Phone: +43 662 8743460
- Address: Giselakai 3-5, 5020 Salzburg, Austria
- Rating: 5 stars

Boutique Hotel am Dom

Located in the heart of Salzburg's old town, Boutique Hotel am Dom offers a charming and intimate stay. This small boutique hotel features individually decorated rooms that combine historic elements with modern comfort.

- Price: From €140 per night
- Phone: +43 662 842765

- Address: Goldgasse 17, 5020 Salzburg, Austria
- Rating: 4.5 stars

ArtHotel Blaue Gans

ArtHotel Blaue Gans, situated on the famous Getreidegasse, is Salzburg's oldest inn, dating back over 650 years. This boutique hotel uniquely combines contemporary art with historic architecture, offering a cultural and artistic experience.

- Price: From €150 per night
- Phone: +43 662 8424910
- Address: Getreidegasse 41-43, 5020 Salzburg, Austria
- Rating: 5 stars

Unique Stays in Innsbruck

NALA Individuellhotel

NALA Individuellhotel offers an artistic and unique experience with its individually designed rooms. Located close to the old town, the hotel provides easy access to Innsbruck's attractions and offers amenities like a beautiful garden and a fitness center.

- Price: From €130 per night
- Phone: +43 512 584444
- Address: Müllerstraße 15, 6020 Innsbruck, Austria
- Rating: 4.5 stars

aDLERS Hotel

aDLERS Hotel is a modern and stylish hotel offering panoramic views of Innsbruck and the surrounding Alps. The hotel features chic rooms, a rooftop bar, and a restaurant, all with stunning views.

- Price: From €150 per night
- Phone: +43 512 563100
- Address: Brunecker Str. 1, 6020 Innsbruck, Austria

- Rating: 5 stars

The Penz Hotel

The Penz Hotel combines contemporary luxury with a central location in Innsbruck. It offers modern rooms, a rooftop bar, and an extensive breakfast buffet with panoramic views of the city.

- Price: From €140 per night
- Phone: +43 512 5756570
- Address: Adolf-Pichler-Platz 3, 6020 Innsbruck, Austria
- Rating: 5 stars

Unique Stays in Graz

Schlossberghotel – Das Kunsthotel

Schlossberghotel – Das Kunsthotel is a unique boutique hotel located at the foot of the Schlossberg hill. The hotel features a collection of contemporary art, individually decorated rooms, and a rooftop terrace with stunning views of Graz.

- Price: From €160 per night
- Phone: +43 316 80760
- Address: Kaiser-Franz-Josef-Kai 30, 8010 Graz, Austria
- Rating: 5 stars

Augarten Art Hotel

Augarten Art Hotel is a modern design hotel featuring a large collection of contemporary art. Located near the city center, the hotel offers stylish rooms, an outdoor pool, and a fitness center.

- Price: From €150 per night
- Phone: +43 316 2080
- Address: Schönaugasse 53, 8010 Graz, Austria
- Rating: 5 stars

HEALTH AND SAFETY

Medical Services and Emergencies

Accessing Medical Services

Austria has a robust healthcare system that offers excellent medical services to both residents and visitors. The system is a blend of public and private healthcare providers, ensuring comprehensive coverage for all.

Public Healthcare: Most residents are covered by public health insurance, which grants access to a broad range of medical services, including visits to general practitioners (GPs), specialists, hospitals, and emergency care. The public system is well-regulated and offers high-quality care.

Private Healthcare: Private health insurance is also available and can cover additional services such as private hospital rooms and quicker access to specialists. Many residents opt for supplementary private insurance to enhance their healthcare experience.

Finding a Doctor:

General Practitioners (GPs): Finding a GP in Austria is straightforward. You can ask at your hotel, the local tourist information center, or consult the Austrian Medical Chamber's website. GPs are your first point of contact for medical issues and can refer you to specialists if needed.

Specialists: To see a specialist, you usually need a referral from a GP. However, some specialists can be consulted directly. Again, resources like the Austrian Medical Chamber's website can help you find a specialist.

Pharmacies (Apotheke): Pharmacies are ubiquitous in Austria. They not only dispense prescription medications but also offer over-the-counter drugs and medical advice. Many pharmacies have extended hours, and there is always a 24-hour pharmacy available in every region.

Hospitals:

Austria is home to numerous well-equipped hospitals, including general hospitals, university hospitals, and specialized clinics. Major cities like Vienna, Graz, and Innsbruck have hospitals that provide advanced medical care with state-of-the-art facilities.

Handling Emergencies

Emergency Numbers:

In Austria, emergency services are efficient and accessible. Here are the key numbers you need to know:

- General Emergency Number: 112 (can be dialed for any emergency)
- Ambulance and Medical Emergency: 144
- Police: 133
- Fire Brigade: 122

What to Do in an Emergency:

1. Stay Calm: First and foremost, try to remain calm and assess the situation.

2. Call for Help: Dial 112 or 144 for medical emergencies. Be prepared to provide clear information about the nature of the emergency, your location, and any other relevant details.

3. Follow Instructions: Follow the instructions given by the emergency operator until help arrives.

Emergency Services:

Ambulance Services: Austria has efficient ambulance services that can quickly provide on-site medical assistance and transport to hospitals if necessary.

Emergency Departments: Hospitals have emergency departments (Notaufnahme) that are open 24/7 to handle urgent medical cases. These departments are well-staffed with experienced medical professionals ready to provide immediate care.

Medical Insurance

Essential Coverage: It is highly recommended that visitors to Austria have travel insurance that covers medical expenses, including emergency care and repatriation if necessary. This ensures you are covered for any unexpected medical costs.

European Health Insurance Card (EHIC): EU/EEA citizens can use their EHIC to access public healthcare services at a reduced cost or sometimes for free. This card provides access to medically necessary, state-provided healthcare during a temporary stay.

Pharmacies and Medications

Pharmacies (Apotheke):

Pharmacies are widely available and offer a range of services. Pharmacists can provide over-the-counter medications, advice on minor health issues, and guidance on prescription medications.

Prescription Medications:

If you need a prescription, you can obtain it from a GP or specialist. If you're running low on a medication you regularly take, it's a good idea to bring your prescription or a note from your home doctor.

Personal Recommendations

Keep Important Information Handy: Always carry important health information with you, such as a list of medications you are taking, allergy information, and emergency contact details.

Language Tips: While many healthcare providers speak English, it can be helpful to know a few key medical terms in German or use a translation app if needed.

Safety Tips for Travelers

Stay Aware of Your Surroundings

Austria is generally a very safe country, but like anywhere else, it's always good to stay aware of your surroundings. Petty theft can occur, especially in crowded tourist areas. Keep your valuables secure and be mindful of your bags and wallets. When you're in bustling spots like the Vienna State Opera or the historic centers of Salzburg and Innsbruck, a little vigilance goes a long way. Consider using a money belt or neck pouch to keep your important documents and money safe, ensuring that your essentials are always close to you and out of reach of pickpockets.

Health and Emergency Numbers

Knowing the local emergency numbers can be a lifesaver. In Austria, dial 112 for any emergency, or 144 specifically for medical emergencies. The police can be reached at 133 and the fire brigade at 122. It's also a good idea to carry a health card. If you're from the EU, bring your European Health Insurance Card (EHIC), which can provide access to necessary medical treatment. For non-EU visitors, ensure you have comprehensive travel insurance that covers medical expenses, including emergency care and repatriation if necessary.

Public Transport Tips

Austria's public transport system is excellent, but here are some tips to make your travel smoother. Always validate your public transport tickets before boarding. Inspectors frequently check tickets, and fines for not having a valid ticket can be steep. If you're taking the U-Bahn in Vienna or a bus through the scenic Tyrol region, staying on schedule is important. Trains and buses in Austria are known for their punctuality, so make sure to arrive at the station a bit early to ensure you don't miss your ride.

Respect Local Customs and Laws

Respecting local customs and laws is important to ensure a smooth and respectful experience. Austrians generally dress conservatively, so when visiting churches or formal places, dress appropriately. Smoking is banned in many public places, including restaurants and bars, so pay attention to no-smoking signs. Additionally, Austria is very eco-conscious. You'll find recycling bins everywhere, and it's expected that you separate your waste accordingly. Participating in local recycling practices is a small but significant way to show respect for Austrian culture.

Outdoor Activities Safety

If you're planning to enjoy Austria's great outdoors, keep these tips in mind. The weather in the mountains can change rapidly, so always check the forecast and be prepared with appropriate clothing. Stick to marked trails when hiking or skiing to ensure your safety and help preserve the natural environment. If you're heading out for activities like hiking or skiing, always let someone know your plans and expected return time. This ensures that someone is aware of your whereabouts in case of an emergency.

Communication

Language barriers can be minimized with a few handy tips. Knowing a few basic German phrases can go a long way. Austrians appreciate the effort, even if many speak English. A simple "Danke" (thank you) or "Bitte" (please) can make interactions smoother. Use mobile apps like Google Translate to help communicate if you get stuck. Having a translation app handy can bridge any communication gaps and make your interactions more pleasant and effective.

Money and Banking

Handling money in a foreign country can sometimes be tricky. While cards are widely accepted, it's always good to carry some cash, especially in smaller towns or rural areas where card machines might be less common. Use ATMs located in banks rather than standalone ones to avoid higher fees and the risk of skimming devices. This practice ensures that your transactions are secure and that you have access to cash when needed.

Local Cuisine and Water

Enjoying local food and drink is one of the joys of travel. Don't miss out on trying Austrian delicacies like Wiener Schnitzel, Apfelstrudel, and Sachertorte. Tap water in Austria is safe to drink and of high quality, so you can refill your water bottle as needed. Carry a refillable bottle to stay hydrated throughout your travels, and enjoy the delicious and safe local cuisine without worry.

MONEY MATTERS

Currency and Exchange

Austria is part of the Eurozone, so the official currency is the Euro. The Euro is divided into 100 cents, and you'll find coins in denominations of 1, 2, 5, 10, 20, and 50 cents, as well as €1 and €2 coins. Banknotes come in €5, €10, €20, €50, €100, €200, and €500 denominations. The Euro is widely accepted throughout Austria, so you won't have to worry about currency issues while traveling within the country.

Where to Exchange Money

While it's convenient to use ATMs, you might also need to exchange cash at some point. Here are some options:

Banks: Austrian banks are reliable places to exchange money. They usually offer competitive rates, but keep in mind their operating hours, typically Monday to Friday from 8 AM to 3 PM, with a longer break at lunchtime.

Exchange Offices: Currency exchange offices can be found in airports, train stations, and city centers. They are convenient but often charge higher fees and offer less favorable rates than banks.

ATMs: ATMs are widely available and are a convenient way to withdraw Euros directly. Just be aware of any fees your home bank might charge for international withdrawals.

Using ATMs

ATMs (Geldautomaten) are plentiful in Austria, and using them is straightforward. Most accept international debit and credit cards (look for symbols like Visa, MasterCard, and Maestro). Here's how to make the most of ATMs:

Withdraw Cash: ATMs provide instructions in multiple languages. Choose English and follow the steps to withdraw cash. The machine will dispense Euros.

Know Your Fees: Your home bank may charge fees for international withdrawals. Additionally, some ATMs charge their own fees. It's a good idea to withdraw larger amounts less frequently to minimize fees.

Safety Tips: Use ATMs located in well-lit, busy areas, such as inside banks or shopping centers, to ensure your safety.

Credit and Debit Cards

Credit and debit cards are widely accepted in Austria, especially in urban areas and larger establishments. However, smaller shops, cafes, and rural locations may prefer cash. Here are a few tips:

Inform Your Bank: Notify your bank of your travel plans to avoid any issues with card transactions being flagged as suspicious.

Chip and PIN: Austria uses the chip and PIN system for card transactions. Make sure your card has a chip and you know your PIN.

Contactless Payments: Many places accept contactless payments, which can be a convenient way to pay for small purchases quickly.

Handling Cash

While cards are widely accepted, having some cash on hand is always a good idea. It's especially useful for small purchases, tipping, and places that don't accept cards. Here's how to handle cash in Austria:

Carry Small Denominations: Keep a mix of small denominations for everyday expenses. It's easier for small vendors to provide change.

Secure Your Cash: Use a money belt or a secure bag to keep your cash safe, especially in crowded areas.

Currency Exchange Rates

Currency exchange rates fluctuate, so it's a good idea to check the current rate before exchanging money. You can find the latest rates online, at banks, or via currency converter apps. Keeping an eye on the rates helps you get the best deal when exchanging your money.

Budgeting Tips

Plan Ahead and Book Early

One of the best ways to save money is to plan your trip well in advance. Booking flights, accommodation, and even some attractions early can secure lower prices. Keep an eye out for deals and discounts on travel websites and consider setting up price alerts to get the best rates.

Travel Off-Peak

Austria is a year-round destination, but traveling during off-peak seasons (late fall and early spring) can save you a lot of money. Prices for flights, hotels, and even some attractions tend to be lower when fewer tourists are around. Plus, you'll enjoy a more relaxed experience with fewer crowds.

Use Public Transport

Austria has an excellent public transport system, which is both efficient and affordable. Instead of renting a car or taking taxis, use trams, buses, and trains to get around. Consider purchasing a public transport pass if you plan to use it frequently. In Vienna, for instance, the Vienna City Card offers unlimited travel on public transport and discounts on many attractions.

Stay in Budget Accommodations

While Austria has many luxury hotels, there are also plenty of budget-friendly options. Look for hostels, guesthouses, and budget hotels that offer comfortable stays at lower prices. Websites like Airbnb can also provide affordable lodging options, especially if you don't mind staying a bit outside the city center.

Eat Like a Local

Dining out can be expensive, but you can save money by eating like a local. Look for local markets, street food vendors, and budget-friendly restaurants. Austrian supermarkets also have a great selection of ready-to-eat meals and snacks. Don't forget to try local specialties like Wiener Schnitzel, Apfelstrudel, and Sachertorte at affordable eateries.

Take Advantage of Free Attractions

Austria offers many free or low-cost attractions. Take a walk through the historic streets of Vienna, visit the stunning lakes in the Salzkammergut region, or hike in the Austrian Alps. Many cities offer free walking tours where you can learn about the history and culture from knowledgeable guides. Additionally, some museums and galleries offer free admission on certain days of the month.

Use Discount Passes

Many cities in Austria offer discount passes for tourists. The Vienna Pass, for example, provides free entry to over 60 attractions, including the Schönbrunn Palace and the Giant Ferris Wheel, and allows you to skip the lines. These passes can be a great way to save money if you plan to visit multiple attractions.

Limit Souvenir Spending

Souvenirs can quickly add up, so be mindful of your spending. Instead of buying expensive items, consider small, meaningful souvenirs like local snacks, postcards, or small crafts. If you're looking for something unique, visit local markets where you can often find handmade goods at reasonable prices.

Manage Your Money Wisely

Keep an eye on your budget by tracking your expenses daily. Use a budgeting app to monitor your spending and ensure you're staying within your limits. Also, be aware of any foreign transaction fees that your bank may charge and consider using a travel credit card that offers no foreign transaction fees.

Travel Insurance

While it might seem like an extra expense, travel insurance can save you money in the long run by covering unexpected costs like medical emergencies, trip cancellations, and lost luggage. It's a small investment for peace of mind during your travels.

Sample Budget

Budget Traveler

Accommodation:

- Hostel Dorm Bed: €20-30 per night
- Budget Hotel: €40-60 per night

Food:

- Breakfast: Included at most hostels and budget hotels, or €5 at a local cafe
- Lunch: €5-10 (street food or inexpensive restaurant)
- Dinner: €10-15 (local eateries or budget restaurants)

Transportation:

- Public Transport Pass: €10 per day (or €40-50 per week)

- Intercity Train/Bus: €20-40 per trip

Activities:

- Free walking tours: €0 (tip appreciated)
- Museum or Attraction Entry: €5-10
- Miscellaneous (souvenirs, etc.): €5-10 per day

Total: €50-80 per day

Mid-Range Traveler

Accommodation:

- Mid-Range Hotel: €80-120 per night
- Airbnb/Guesthouse: €70-100 per night

Food:

- Breakfast: Included or €5-10 at a cafe
- Lunch: €10-20 (mid-range restaurant)
- Dinner: €20-30 (nice restaurant)

Transportation:

- Public Transport Pass: €10 per day
- Taxi Rides: €10-20 per ride (short distances)
- Intercity Train/Bus: €30-60 per trip

Activities:

- Guided Tours: €20-40
- Museum or Attraction Entry: €10-15
- Miscellaneous: €10-15 per day

Total: €100-150 per day

Luxury Traveler

Accommodation:

- Luxury Hotel: €200-500+ per night
- High-End Airbnb: €150-300 per night

Food:

- Breakfast: €20-30 (luxury hotel breakfast or high-end cafe)
- Lunch: €30-50 (fine dining restaurant)
- Dinner: €50-100+ (gourmet restaurant)

Transportation:

- Private Transfers/Taxis: €30-50 per ride
- Rental Car: €50-100 per day
- Intercity Train/Bus: €60-100 (first-class tickets)

Activities:

- Private Tours: €100-200+
- Museum or Attraction Entry: €20-30 (including special exhibits)
- Spa/Wellness: €50-150 per session
- Miscellaneous: €20-50 per day

Total: €300-600+ per day

LANGUAGE AND PHRASES

Basic German Phrases

Greetings and Polite Expressions

- Hello: Hallo
- Good morning: Guten Morgen
- Good afternoon: Guten Tag
- Good evening: Guten Abend
- Goodbye: Auf Wiedersehen
- See you later: Bis später
- Please: Bitte
- Thank you: Danke
- You're welcome: Bitte schön / Gern geschehen
- Yes: Ja
- No: Nein
- Excuse me: Entschuldigung
- Sorry: Es tut mir leid

Common Questions

- Do you speak English?: Sprechen Sie Englisch?
- Where is the bathroom?: Wo ist die Toilette?
- How much does this cost?: Wie viel kostet das?
- Can you help me?: Können Sie mir helfen?
- What time is it?: Wie spät ist es?

Directions and Transportation

- Where is the train station?: Wo ist der Bahnhof?
- I need a taxi: Ich brauche ein Taxi
- Is this seat taken?: Ist dieser Platz frei?
- Left: Links

- Right: Rechts
- Straight ahead: Geradeaus
- Here: Hier
- There: Dort

Dining and Shopping

- I would like...: Ich hätte gern...
- The bill, please: Die Rechnung, bitte
- Do you have a menu in English?: Haben Sie eine Speisekarte auf Englisch?
- I'm allergic to...: Ich bin allergisch gegen...
- How much is this?: Wie viel kostet das?
- Can I try this on?: Kann ich das anprobieren?

Emergencies

- I need a doctor: Ich brauche einen Arzt
- Call the police: Rufen Sie die Polizei
- Help!: Hilfe!
- I'm lost: Ich habe mich verlaufen
- I need help: Ich brauche Hilfe

Numbers

- One: Eins
- Two: Zwei
- Three: Drei
- Four: Vier
- Five: Fünf
- Six: Sechs
- Seven: Sieben
- Eight: Acht
- Nine: Neun
- Ten: Zehn

Language Resources

Duolingo

Duolingo offers a comprehensive German course that is suitable for beginners and intermediate learners. It uses gamified lessons to make learning fun and engaging.

Babbel

Babbel provides structured German lessons focusing on practical conversation skills, vocabulary, and grammar. It's designed for learners at all levels.

Rosetta Stone

Rosetta Stone is a well-known language learning platform that offers immersive German lessons using a combination of images, text, and audio.

Leo.org

Leo.org is a popular online dictionary that provides translations, definitions, and usage examples for German words and phrases.

Linguee

Linguee combines a dictionary with a search engine to find translations and example sentences from real texts, helping you understand word usage in context.

DAY TRIPS AND EXCURSIONS

From Vienna to Wachau Valley

First things first, getting to the Wachau Valley from Vienna is a breeze. You can take a train from Vienna's main train station (Wien Hauptbahnhof) to Krems an der Donau, which is the gateway to the valley. The train journey is about 1 hour and costs around €18 for a one-way ticket. Trains run frequently, so you have plenty of options for departure times.

Once you arrive in Krems, you can either rent a bike, which is a popular option, or use the local buses to get around. If you're up for some cycling, there are several rental shops near the train station where you can rent a bike for the day for about €15-20. Biking along the Danube River is an unforgettable experience with breathtaking views at every turn.

Exploring the Wachau Valley

Start in Krems:

Begin your adventure in the charming town of Krems. Stroll through its old town, a UNESCO World Heritage site, and admire the beautiful medieval architecture. Don't miss the Kunsthalle Krems, an art gallery that often hosts fascinating exhibitions. Entrance to the Kunsthalle is about €9.

Visit Dürnstein:

Next, head to the quaint village of Dürnstein, about 8 km from Krems. You can bike there along the scenic route or take a local bus. Dürnstein is famous for its striking blue church tower and the ruins of Dürnstein Castle, where Richard the Lionheart was imprisoned. Climb up to the ruins for a small fee of €2.50, and you'll be rewarded with spectacular views of the Danube and the valley below.

Wine Tasting in Weissenkirchen:

After exploring Dürnstein, continue your journey to Weissenkirchen, another picturesque village nestled among vineyards. This area is known for its exceptional white wines, especially Grüner Veltliner and Riesling. Visit one of the local wineries for a tasting session. A typical wine tasting costs around €10-15, and it's a delightful way to experience the region's flavors. I highly recommend Weingut Jamek, a family-run winery with a lovely tasting room and excellent wines.

Lunch at a Heuriger:

For lunch, stop at a traditional Heuriger, a local wine tavern, where you can enjoy hearty Austrian cuisine and locally produced wine. Heuriger Höllmüller in Weissenkirchen is a fantastic choice, offering delicious dishes like Wiener Schnitzel and Brettljause (a platter of cold meats, cheeses, and spreads). Expect to spend about €20-25 per person for a satisfying meal and a glass of wine.

Exploring Melk Abbey:

End your day with a visit to the magnificent Melk Abbey. From Weissenkirchen, you can take a bus or continue cycling to Melk, about 20 km away. Melk Abbey is a stunning baroque masterpiece perched on a hill overlooking the Danube. The entrance fee is €14.50, and it includes a guided tour of the abbey's opulent interior, beautiful gardens, and the impressive library.

From Salzburg to Hallstatt

Our journey begins in Salzburg, and there are a couple of ways to reach Hallstatt. The most scenic and convenient route is by train and ferry. Head to Salzburg's main train station (Salzburg Hauptbahnhof) and catch a train to Attnang-Puchheim. From there, you'll transfer to a local train that will take you to the town of Hallstatt. The entire journey by train takes around 2.5 to 3 hours and costs about €20-30 one way.

Once you arrive at Hallstatt train station, you'll hop on a charming ferry that crosses the lake to the village. The ferry ride is only about 10 minutes and costs €3 per person. The moment you see Hallstatt from the water, you'll understand why this village is so beloved – the view is simply breathtaking.

Start your day by exploring the heart of Hallstatt – the Market Square. This picturesque square is surrounded by pastel-colored buildings and quaint shops. Take your time to wander around, grab a coffee at one of the cafes, and soak in the enchanting atmosphere. The square is also a great place to pick up some local souvenirs.

Next, head to the Hallstatt Museum to get a deep dive into the rich history of this village. The museum showcases artifacts from the prehistoric salt mines that Hallstatt is famous for, along with exhibits on the village's development through the ages. Admission to the museum is €10 for adults. It's a small price to pay to appreciate the cultural heritage that makes Hallstatt so unique.

For lunch, I recommend heading to one of the lakeside restaurants. Restaurant im Seehotel Grüner Baum is a fantastic option. Here, you can enjoy delicious Austrian cuisine with a stunning view of the lake. Expect to spend around €25-30 per person for a hearty meal with a drink. Be sure to try the local fish dishes – they're incredibly fresh and tasty.

After lunch, it's time for a bit of adventure. Hallstatt's salt mines are among the oldest in the world, and a tour is a must-do. Take the funicular up to the entrance, which costs €18 round trip. The guided tour of the mines is €30, but it's worth every penny. You'll learn about the ancient techniques used to mine salt and even slide down a wooden chute used by miners – it's a blast!

Before heading back down, make sure to visit the Skywalk viewing platform. It's a short walk from the salt mine entrance and offers panoramic views of Hallstatt and the lake from 350 meters above. The views are absolutely stunning and make for great photo opportunities.

If you have time before heading back to Salzburg, check out the Bone House in St. Michael's Chapel. This unique site houses over 1,200 skulls, many of which are painted and date back centuries. The entry fee is just €1.50. It's a fascinating glimpse into local traditions and the community's approach to mortality.

From Innsbruck to Neuschwanstein Castle

Our journey begins in Innsbruck, where you can catch a train to Füssen, Germany. The trip involves a transfer at either Garmisch-Partenkirchen or Munich, depending on the schedule. The train ride offers stunning alpine views and takes about 2.5 to 3 hours. Round-trip tickets typically cost around €50-70. From Füssen, you can take a short bus ride (bus number 73 or 78) to Hohenschwangau, where the castle is located. The bus ride costs about €2.50 each way.

Once you arrive in Hohenschwangau, you'll immediately be captivated by the stunning scenery. The village is charming, with beautiful views of the surrounding mountains and lakes. Head to the ticket center to purchase your entry ticket for Neuschwanstein Castle. I recommend booking your tickets in advance online to avoid long queues. The guided tour of the castle costs €17.50 for adults.

There are a few ways to get to the castle itself: a shuttle bus (€3.50 round trip), a horse-drawn carriage (€6 uphill, €3 downhill), or by walking. If you're up for it, I highly recommend the walk. It's a gentle 30-40 minute uphill hike through beautiful woods with glimpses of the castle along the way. It's the perfect warm-up for the adventure ahead.

Once you reach the castle, join the guided tour to explore the interior. The tour lasts about 35 minutes and takes you through the opulent rooms that King Ludwig II had decorated. The Throne Room and the Singer's Hall are particularly impressive, with their ornate designs and breathtaking views of the surrounding countryside. The tour is filled with fascinating stories about the eccentric king and the castle's history.

After the tour, take a short walk to Marienbrücke, the famous bridge that offers the best views of Neuschwanstein Castle. The panoramic view from the bridge is absolutely stunning and perfect for photographs. It's a bit of a climb to get there, but the effort is well worth it.

For lunch, head back down to Hohenschwangau and stop at one of the local restaurants. Schlossrestaurant Neuschwanstein offers a lovely dining experience with a view of the castle. Enjoy some hearty Bavarian dishes like sausages, pretzels, and schnitzel. Expect to spend around €20-25 per person for a meal and a drink.

If you have time after lunch, consider visiting Hohenschwangau Castle, which is just a short walk away. This castle was the childhood home of King Ludwig II and offers another fascinating glimpse into Bavarian history. The entry fee is €21, and the tour lasts about 45 minutes.

CONCLUSION

As we come to the end of this travel guide, I want to extend a heartfelt thank you for choosing this guide to help you navigate your journey through Austria. It's been a pleasure sharing my knowledge and tips with you, and I hope this guide has inspired and equipped you for an unforgettable adventure.

From the historic streets of Vienna to the stunning landscapes of the Wachau Valley, Austria is a country that offers a diverse array of experiences. We've explored hidden gems like the serene town of Hallstatt, delved into off-the-beaten-path adventures such as hiking in the Rax mountains, and discovered ways to avoid tourist traps to ensure a more authentic experience. Each destination in Austria holds its own unique charm, and I'm excited for you to uncover these treasures for yourself.

Remember to plan ahead and book early to secure the best deals and avoid disappointment. Embrace the local culture by dining where the locals eat, exploring lesser-known attractions, and engaging with the friendly Austrian people.

As you travel, keep in mind the tips and insights shared in this guide. Use public transport to explore the cities efficiently, carry some cash for smaller purchases, and always have a reusable water bottle to stay hydrated. Most importantly, don't forget to venture beyond the main tourist spots to discover the true essence of Austria.

I hope this guide has been more than just a resource but a companion in your planning process. Thank you for trusting me to be a part of your travel preparations. Your choice to use this guide has given me the opportunity to share my love for Austria and its many wonders.

APPENDIX

Emergency Numbers and Health Services

Emergency Contacts:

- General Emergency Number: 112 (for any emergency)
- Medical Emergency/Ambulance: 144
- Police: 133
- Fire Brigade: 122

Health Services:

Hospitals: Austria has numerous well-equipped hospitals in major cities and towns. Some prominent ones include:

- Vienna: AKH Vienna General Hospital
- Salzburg: University Hospital Salzburg
- Innsbruck: University Hospital Innsbruck

Pharmacies (Apotheke): Available widely, with some open 24/7. Look for signs indicating the nearest pharmacy on duty.

Travel Insurance: Highly recommended to cover medical expenses and emergencies. EU/EEA citizens can use the EHIC card.

Currency and Banking

Currency:

The official currency is the Euro (€).

Banking:

ATMs (Geldautomaten): Widely available in cities and towns.

Credit and Debit Cards: Widely accepted, but it's advisable to carry some cash for smaller establishments.

Currency Exchange: Available at banks, airports, and exchange offices. Avoid exchanging large amounts at airports due to higher fees.

Language and Communication

Official Language: German (with Austrian German dialects).

Basic Phrases:

- Hello: Hallo
- Thank you: Danke
- Please: Bitte
- Excuse me: Entschuldigung
- Do you speak English?: Sprechen Sie Englisch?

Language Resources:

- Online Courses: Duolingo, Babbel, Rosetta Stone
- Dictionaries: Leo.org, Linguee
- Language Exchange: Tandem, HelloTalk

Transport and Travel

Public Transport:

Vienna: Excellent public transport including U-Bahn (subway), trams, and buses. Vienna City Card offers unlimited travel.

Innsbruck, Salzburg, Graz: Well-developed networks of trams and buses.

Intercity Travel:

Trains: Efficient and comfortable. ÖBB (Austrian Federal Railways) and Westbahn are the main providers.

Buses: FlixBus and local bus services offer extensive routes.

Driving:

Requirements: Valid driver's license, insurance, and vehicle documents. International Driving Permit (IDP) recommended for non-EU visitors.

Roads: Well-maintained, but be aware of tolls on highways and the need for a vignette (toll sticker).

Cultural Etiquette and Customs

Greetings:

- A firm handshake is common.
- Use formal titles (Herr/Frau) unless invited to use first names.

Dining:

- Wait to be seated in restaurants.
- It is customary to tip by rounding up the bill or leaving 5-10%.

Local Customs:

- Respect quiet hours, typically from 10 PM to 7 AM.
- Recycling is important; follow local guidelines for waste separation.

Must-See Attractions

Vienna:

- Schönbrunn Palace
- St. Stephen's Cathedral
- Belvedere Palace
- MuseumsQuartier

Salzburg:

- Hohensalzburg Fortress
- Mozart's Birthplace
- Mirabell Palace and Gardens

Innsbruck:

- Golden Roof
- Nordkette Mountain Range
- Ambras Castle

Graz:

- Schlossberg and Clock Tower
- Kunsthaus Graz
- Eggenberg Palace

Hallstatt:

- Hallstatt Salt Mine
- Hallstätter See
- Skywalk Hallstatt Viewing Platform

Outdoor Activities

Hiking:

- Popular in the Alps and regions like the Rax and Schneeberg mountains.
- Well-marked trails suitable for all levels.

Skiing:

- Renowned ski resorts include Kitzbühel, St. Anton, and Zell am See.
- Winter season runs from December to April.

Cycling:

- The Danube Cycle Path is a scenic and popular route.
- Rent bikes from local shops or at train stations.

GLOSSARY

- Almdudler:

A popular Austrian soft drink made from herbal extracts. It's often referred to as the "national drink" of Austria.

- Apfelstrudel:

A traditional Austrian dessert consisting of thinly stretched dough filled with spiced apples, raisins, sugar, and breadcrumbs.

- Apotheke:

Pharmacy. These are widely available in Austria and provide both prescription and over-the-counter medications.

- Austrian Airlines:

The flag carrier of Austria, providing both domestic and international flights.

- Beisl:

A type of traditional Austrian pub or tavern where local cuisine and drinks are served.

- Berliner:

A doughnut filled with jam or custard, often enjoyed as a sweet treat.

- Berg:

Mountain. Austria is known for its beautiful mountain ranges, particularly the Alps.

- Bundesland:

Federal state. Austria is divided into nine federal states, each with its own unique characteristics.

- Dachstein:

A prominent mountain range in the Northern Limestone Alps, known for its scenic beauty and opportunities for outdoor activities.

- Danube River (Donau):

One of Europe's major rivers, flowing through Austria and offering scenic views, particularly in the Wachau Valley.

- Edelweiss:

A white flower that grows in the alpine regions of Austria and is a symbol of the Alps.

- Eisriesenwelt:

The world's largest ice cave, located near Werfen in Austria.

- Fledermaus:

Bat. Also the title of a famous operetta by Johann Strauss II, "Die Fledermaus."

- Funicular (Seilbahn):

A cable railway used to transport people up steep slopes, common in mountainous regions of Austria.

- Glockenspiel:

A musical instrument consisting of a set of tuned keys, arranged in the fashion of the keyboard of a piano.

- Grüner Veltliner:

A type of white wine grape grown primarily in Austria, known for producing a light, crisp wine.

- Heuriger:

A wine tavern in Austria where local winemakers serve their new wine and traditional Austrian food.

- Hofburg:

The former imperial palace in Vienna, which now houses several museums and the Austrian National Library.

- Kaiserschmarrn:

A fluffy, shredded pancake, typically served with fruit compote or powdered sugar.

- Krapfen:

A type of Austrian doughnut filled with apricot jam or custard, traditionally eaten during Carnival.

- Mozartkugel:

A famous Austrian confection made of marzipan, nougat, and dark chocolate, named after Wolfgang Amadeus Mozart.

- Müesli:

A popular breakfast dish in Austria, consisting of rolled oats, nuts, seeds, and fresh or dried fruits, typically served with milk or yogurt.

- Naschmarkt:

A famous market in Vienna offering a wide range of food products, from fresh produce to international delicacies.

- Neujahrskonzert:

The Vienna New Year's Concert, a classical music concert performed by the Vienna Philharmonic Orchestra on January 1st each year.

- ÖBB:

Austrian Federal Railways, the national railway company of Austria, providing extensive train services throughout the country and beyond.

- Ötztal:

A valley in Tyrol, Austria, known for its winter sports and hiking trails.

- Pfand:

Deposit. In Austria, many bottles and cans come with a deposit that is refunded when the container is returned.

- Prater:

A large public park in Vienna, home to the famous Giant Ferris Wheel (Riesenrad).

- Radler:

A refreshing drink made by mixing beer with lemonade, popular in Austria during the summer.

- Rathaus:

Town hall. Many Austrian cities have a Rathaus, which often serves as an important landmark.

- Sachertorte:

A famous chocolate cake from Vienna, traditionally served with whipped cream.

- Salzburger Nockerl:

A sweet, fluffy soufflé-like dessert from Salzburg.

- Schloss:

Castle or palace. Austria is home to many historic and beautiful castles and palaces.

- Tafelspitz:

A traditional Austrian dish of boiled beef, typically served with horseradish and apple sauce.

- U-Bahn:

The underground metro system in Vienna, providing efficient public transportation throughout the city.

- Unter den Linden:

While this is a famous boulevard in Berlin, the phrase is also used in Austria to refer to promenades lined with lime trees.

- Volksoper:

The Vienna Volksoper is a major opera house in Vienna, offering a variety of operas, musicals, and ballets.

- Vignette:

A toll sticker required for driving on Austrian motorways. It must be displayed on the windshield.

- Zillertal:

A valley in the Tyrol region, known for its skiing, hiking, and stunning alpine scenery.

- Zug:

Train. Austria has an extensive and efficient train network that connects major cities and regions.

Printed in Dunstable, United Kingdom